FLEMMING CHRISTENSEN

The Enneagram in Relationships

**THINK ABOUT
IT**

FOREWORD

If you are reading this book, you are probably interested either in the Enneagram or in the interactions between yourself and those with whom you share a close relationship – or perhaps both. People starting an introductory course in the Enneagram are very likely to be interested in learning more about themselves and those around them, such as their family, friends and colleagues, and are keen to be able to make as much practical use of this knowledge as possible. When entering into a close relationship – whether professional or romantic – people generally hope that they can get it to flourish as much as possible, that they can deal with any conflicts that may arise, and that they can develop themselves to the extent that they are able to chart the development of the relation- ship itself.

This book covers the Enneagram Types and their interactions; if, however, you are not yet familiar with the Enneagram, this book will nonetheless provide you with inspiration in working out how you and your partner can yourselves in your relationship. The book can, more specifically, be used as a pathway to achieving an understanding of the Types as we review the most fundamental emotional patterns characteristic of each of the nine Enneagram Types.

If you are already familiar with the Enneagram, you can look forward to a further elaboration of the genesis of each Type and the emotional structures around which it is built during very early childhood. As someone with knowledge of the Enneagram, you have doubtless asked yourself, "How can it be that, on the one hand, Type 2 has such difficulties dealing with a 'no' or even setting boundaries in close relationships – yet, on the other hand, Type 8 finds it extremely easy to accept a 'no' and to set boundaries in close relationships? And, conversely, how can it be that Type 2 finds it easy to relate to the other, to have empathy and to build relationships, while this is Type 8's biggest lesson in life?" That is, how are motives created for the individual Types?

When I encountered the theory of Object Relations during my first Part 1 in 1999 at the Enneagram Institute, my teachers Don Richard Riso and Russ Hudson spoke engagingly and clearly about the very early pat- terns of the Types, such that it was extremely obvious why Type 2 finds it so difficult to set boundaries and why Type 8 finds it so simple to set these very boundaries. When I began to teach the Enneagram myself, it was natural to keep this part of the theory in the back of my mind, and it was a simple matter to answer questions about the motives of and in- teractions between the Types, but unlike Don and Russ, who included the theory of Object Relations in Part 1 (as their introductory course), I chose to include it in the later courses. This means that the many par- ticipants in THINK ABOUT IT's introductory courses have not received training in Object Relations and therefore lack a deeper understanding of the genesis of the Types, their inner dynamics, and how the Types are mirrored in their close relationships.

I have taught Object Relations for many years and built up my knowl- edge and experience of the subject, which I have now compiled for this book with the intention of producing a clearer description of how we mirror ourselves in our close relationships during our early childhood – and how we thereby develop specific ways of seeing the world alongside the particular skills that dwell so deeply in us that we believe that these entrenched ways of seeing the world, alongside these skills, sum up who we are and describe our personalities. At the same time, we project our- selves in our close relationships when we become adults and "demand" that our partner delivers whatever it was that we did not get as the chil- dren of our close relations (typically our parents).

A "good" answer can therefore be found to the question of why the Types have the motives they do, and it is the depiction of precisely this that is the purpose of this book. In addition to the aforementioned re- view of the Object Relation for each individual Type, I will also sketch out the 45 type pairs and their particular dynamics, as well as the way in which Object Relations play out in close relationships. I hope that you will enjoy reading the book, while simultaneously gaining a deeper in- sight into both yourself and your close relationships.

It should also be pointed out that in fact we "are" not one Type; we just exhibit characteristic traits of a specific Type. At the same time, there are varied attitudes towards the fact that our personality is not a static entity, but is created, developed and formed in interaction with others. It is important to bear this in mind as you begin reading this book; I have devoted a chapter at the end to showing that we must not blindly regard – or identify – ourselves as being a particular Type. Bear this in mind for your own sake and for that of your partner.

Flemming Christensen
June 2018

FOREWORD BY RUSS HUDSON

Anyone studying the Enneagram of Personality will eventually realize that it is an approach to the human condition that utilizes both spiritual practice and psychological understanding. But to get the most benefit from this work, we will need to engage in ongoing practices, but we will also need to go beyond the basic descriptions of types to a more rigorous exploration of the psychological patterns of each type. For this, we can see how the insights of modern psychology do indeed illuminate the ba- sic idea of the nine types and provide means for us to recognize patterns that dominate much of our experience. And particularly, we will discov- er how these patterns impact our relationships.

One of the most useful tools for Enneagram work from contemporary psychotherapy is the concept of Object Relations. The theory of Object Relations began to take shape in the 1940s and 50s and was refined and championed by some of the key thinkers in psychoanalysis— especially D.W. Winnicott, W.R. Fairbairn, Harry Guntrip, and others. The key in- sight that the theory introduced was that our egos are formed and struc- tured by our early relationships. In fact, it could be said that all ego states are relational in nature. For there to be a separate "me" there needs to be an other that defines that separate "me." There needs to be an "other." These psychologists noticed that all ego states had an implicit "other" in them, and that psychological pattern with this other was often superim- posed on current relationships. In other words, we keep reliving those early patterns with the people in our lives now. This led to a refinement of the understanding of "transference" in psychoanalytic relationships and created many methods for healing people from painful and trau- matic patterning in their psyche.

In the 1960s, the American psychologist Margaret Mahler did a long term clinical study on the development of self in the earliest stages of childhood development by observing the stages and processes of this development in a large number of infants. She published her team's findings in the landmark book The Psychological Birth of the Human Infant: Symbiosis and Individuation which supported the earlier theories of object relations with solid research, and led to a greater understand- ing of how our personalities form.

Over the ensuing decades, several different schools of object relations theories arose and developed. One current version of this approach is attachment theory, which looks at the nature of a child's attachment to his or her mother and explores the effects of those different attachment styles in a person's adult life. They each employed somewhat different terminology and emphasis, but they all retained the basic structure of a "self object", "an other object", and "an affect" or emotional energy between the two objects. After many years of clinical use, and with the growing body of research that began with Mahler's work, the theory is well-established in the psychological community worldwide.

There are many books on this topic, but they are almost entirely technical in nature, and are aimed at professionals in counseling and psychotherapy. Those interested in studying the subject at this level could certainly seek out books by the above-mentioned psychologists. Howev- er there have been few books which have helped the lay reader under- stand this fascinating and important topic.

In the early 1990s, I had joined Don Richard Riso in writing about the Enneagram and particularly its correlations with modern psychol- ogy. The Enneagram teacher and psychiatrist Claudio Naranjo had in- troduced connections between the nine Enneagram types and various psychological categories he knew. Don felt this was a fruitful direction and continued to explore different psychological theories to better un- derstand the patterns and function of the Enneagram types. At some point, he and I came across object relations and began to wonder if this powerful perspective could shed light on the Enneagram.

Don had already formed a basic theory of childhood patterns for the types which he introduced in his first book Personality Types. He offered it as a "first shot" at understanding these patterns, but he knew there were limitations in what he had presented.

It was the pioneering work of A.H. Almaas, and his brilliant use of object relations in the development of spiritual awakening that gave us insights into how the patterns my function in the Enneagram types. Similarly, the work of his colleague Alia Johnson helped us to sharpen our ideas about the topic.

We realized that we could not include all of the different theories of object relations in our presentation, knowing that the topic was already somewhat overwhelming for people. Thus we drew from a variety of these schools and found language that we felt best fit with the Ennea- gram view of the psyche. To this end, we developed three concepts for the other object—the nurturing figure, the protective figure, and a com- bination of the both. We noted that the object in the Enneagram pattern had more to do with how a child received particular needs than with a particular person. For example, a child's nurturing needs might come from a grandparent, a nanny, an older sibling, or from the actual father, or from a combination of these. It was not only the biological mother.

Similarly, we settled on names for three basic patterns of object re- lations that were an amalgam of some of the theories we had studied. As is usually the case in object relations theory, these names were de- rived from the dominant affect of the pattern—the emotional energy of it. Thus, we came up with patterns of Attachment, Frustration, and Re- jection. And when these three basic patterns of affect were combined with the three kinds of other object, we had nine patterns, and indeed, found that one of each of these patterns was a key to understanding the psychological underpinnings and current relationship issues for each of the nine types.

Drawing on this work, Flemming Christensen has done a great ser- vice in further making this material accessible to lay readers and looked more extensively at some of the issues that arise from these patterns in our adult relationships. He has presented the material in a systematic way that will help zero in on persistent relationship challenges and suggest solutions for resolving many of the recurrent misunderstanding that arise as we seek to connect with other human beings.

Indeed, rather than go into the specific mechanics of this potentially challenging psychological topic, Flemming explains in clear language the dynamics between each possible combination of Enneagram types. He looks at romantic relationships of course, but also describes other kinds of important relationship—all of which are subject to the same in- teractions of object relations patterns. Wisely, he does not tell us which combinations are "good" or "bad." He focuses on the likely issues and possibilities that can arise in any given relationship. In doing so, he has created a clear and concise manual for navigating the challenges of in- terpersonal dynamics. I suspect that once you have grasped the ideas he is presenting here, you will return to this book many times for guidance in your dealings with other human beings. So take your time, and explore the rich world of relationship with the powerful lens of the Enneagram.

Russ Hudson
Dublin, Ireland
December 9, 2018

STRUCTURE

The Enneagram in Relationships has as its central focal point close relationships (that is, a romantic relationship, a relationship with one's child or a close professional relationship) and therefore draws upon theories from Object Relations and Instincts, as these areas are extremely influ- ential for our ways of being and for how we make demands on our part- ners in close relationships.

Introduction

I begin by explaining why the subject of relationships is important; what consequences follow from ignoring Object Relations and Instincts; what benefits can flow from working with these powerful mechanisms; and the purpose of this book.

Object Relations

In this chapter, we briefly review the theory behind Object Relations and also refer to other sources that examine the theory itself in depth. There is also an explanation of what Object Relations are *not*, alongside a guide to how to understand and work with the basic filter created for us by this branch of psychology. In this context, I would recommend Don Richard Riso and Ross Hudson, *Understanding the Enneagram*, and A. H. Al- maas, *The Pearl Beyond Price*.

About the Nurturing Figure

Here you will learn about the special qualities of the Nurturing Figure, for example the provision of love, necessities and self-worth; this section also outlines the signs that you are in balance and thereby enjoy an es- sential or personified love.

About the Protective Figure

In this chapter you will learn more about the special qualities represent- ed or expressed by the Protective Figure, and thereby consider in detail qualities such as being able to interpret the world accurately, initiate guidelines and express intentions.

The Object Relations for the nine Enneagram Types

In this large chapter, we review the ways that Object Relations manifest themselves in the nine Enneagram Types. You will learn more about the individual characteristics of the Types, how the Object Relation man- ifests itself in all of us regardless of which Type we relate to, and how the three Instincts affect all of us in our Object Relation. I include in this chapter a review of the Relation with respect to close relationships, the special characteristics for the individual Type, and the Instincts. I have included the Instincts as these also play a significant role in close rela- tionships.

Relationships between the Types

Another large chapter, in which I review all the Enneagram Types and ex- plain how a person who relates to one Type interacts with all the others. This approach generates 45 pair-combinations, and you will learn about the dynamics in place when the relationships are secure and in balance and, conversely, when they are insecure and unbalanced. There are also guidelines as to how both Types are able to develop in their relationship.

Closing reflections

The concluding chapter is included to ensure that we avoid becoming too fixated or focussed upon theory. The purpose here is to recognise that we, as individual human beings – and, by extension, also in our close relationships – are much more magical and complex than psychological theories can tell us. My closing remarks are intended to demonstrate that you can manage yourself and your close relationships with the love, wis- dom and care that you deserve.

INTRODUCTION

Why are relationships important?

You constantly mirror yourself in other people and react to the dynam- ic that these projections create in you. It may be that someone smiles warmly at you, making you feel at ease and secure – or the opposite, leading you to wonder why someone is smiling at you: perhaps you think that something is lodged between your teeth, or that you have buttoned up your shirt wrongly.

We cannot help but react to other people's looks, words, actions, hu- mour and so forth, and, particularly when it comes to close relationships such as a sexual partner and others close to us, we have deeply embed- ded patterns that are activated when our partner behaves in a particu- lar way. We can say that your partner is a mirror that fosters, elicits or invokes aspects of your personality that have nothing to do with your partner's actions, but which you usually experience in a particular way that you regard as your partner's responsibility.

These aspects of your personality can be described as that branch of psychology known as "Object Relations", dealing with the relationships you have had with some of the earlier figures in your life, such as your fa- ther and mother or other significant people during your very early child- hood.

What are the negative consequences of not learning about close relationships?

If, in a romantic relationship, you are not aware that your partner is sim- ply activating old patterns in you, you will have a tendency to blame your partner for being too harsh, too practical, too self-obsessed – or, on the other hand, for not listening enough, for not helping enough or for not being attentive enough. Your partner is often just being exactly what your partner should be, but an inner frustration or impotence manifests itself in your perception that if only your partner would change, it would be easier to be you.

Such recriminations can be difficult for your partner to accept, with the result that your partner might begin to react in accordance with their own embedded patterns, demanding that you are less demanding, less aggressive and less censorious – or that you should be more motivated, more enterprising and more accepting and accommodating. Once such a downward spiral is established, it can be difficult to arrest it and re-establish balance – unless both partners recognise that it is not the other that needs to change.

What are the positive consequences of learning about relationships?

In a relationship in which both partners are aware of the mutual dynam- ic within the relationship, it will be easier to take responsibility for your- self rather than blaming the other. This can bring about a virtuous circle, through which you become closer to each other, whilst also developing yourselves as human beings.

When you discover that you are making demands on your partner which are simply needs that were not met during your childhood, you will become more loving, nurturing and accommodating toward your partner – and, in fact, toward yourself as well. In essence, it is necessary in order to be able to develop new skills that, as a child, you had some- one you could mirror yourself in and copy their way of being. If, for what- ever reason, you lacked someone to project yourself onto, you will not have integrated certain skills. By accepting this insight, you can begin to train yourself in the use of these skills rather than requiring your partner to take possession of them or suppress them. Accepting such a consider- able responsibility for yourself will strengthen the relationship even fur- ther, whilst also giving both of you the opportunity to bring to light even more latent issues or needs that have nothing to do with your partner.

When you work with Object Relations, you gain an insight into deep personal patterns and habits, enabling you to loosen your personality's power or grip over your life. You also have a greater chance to forgive the Nurturing and Protective Figures in your life (these may well be your mother and father) because, with your deeper insight into Object Relations, you understand that you interpreted the world through a filter when, for example, you perceived your mother as not loving you – rather than it being a fact that your mother did not love you. In this way, your work with Object Relations will throw into sharp relief the filter from your childhood, or reveal the way in which you interpret the world – which is just one of thousands of ways the world can be interpreted and is there- fore not the only true and definitive way of doing so.

What solutions does this book offer?

In this book, I will provide you with an overview of the types of dynam- ics that arise in close relationships, how to navigate them and how to take greater responsibility for your own patterns, rather than demanding changes in your close relationships themselves.

Object Relations

This chapter is about Object Relations and how they impact upon you generally – and upon the Enneagram Types. The theory behind Object Relations pertains to the fact that we all had a specific relationship with one or several objects (Figures) during our upbringing. This special re- lationship with one or more Figures became a way that we mirrored ourselves in the outside world and thereby began to train ourselves in the skills we saw in the reflection. Many of our skills, convictions and values are thus built upon these early reflections, which is why the the- ory behind Object Relations influenced our previous understanding of the genesis of our personality. I do not intend to deal with the historical background of or developments within the theory of Object Relations, as there are a great many books and online articles providing professional, useful and thoroughly researched descriptions of the theory.

What can you use Object Relations for?

The theory behind Object Relations can furnish you with an understand- ing of the way in which you are caught up in a perception of the Nur- turing and the Protective Figures from your childhood. With this knowl- edge, you can obtain a more precise understanding of whether you have determined the right Type to relate yourself to – and you will also attain a deeper understanding of why you make particular demands of those close to you, such as your sexual partner. Object Relations can also act as an advanced trigger, enabling you to determine when you have veered out of balance and thereby help you back toward presence, curiosity and attentiveness – by which it is understood that when you resort to react- ing according to the entrenched patterns described by the theory behind Object Relations, this can be regarded as a trigger to encourage you to stop and decide whether to react...or not. Object Relations are, then, deeply entrenched patterns, which, when you begin to perceive the pat- terns in your ways of being with other people, can supply you with the renewed desire and energy to progress your narrative about yourself and the new practices that will be effective for you in the future.

The Relationships

There are three different relationships to objects or Figures, and typical- ly you will have one particular relationship to one particular Figure or combination of Figures. Very briefly, we can identify the following rela- tionships:

Rejection
Rejection suggests that, in your experience, you have lacked Nurturing and/or Protective Figures in your childhood. You have therefore not had one or more of these Figures in which to mirror yourself, and you have thus had difficulties in developing the qualities which these Figures rep- resent. If, for example, you have a Rejection-relationship to the Nurturing Figure, you will have lacked qualities such as empathy, sensitivity to others or unconditional love in which to reflect yourself, and you will therefore

not have had a natural role model to learn from. In this connection, it is extremely important to understand that there is a very high probability that you did actually receive love from the Nurturing Figure while you were a child, but that the interpretive filter that determines your perception of how the world functions has ensured that you have not noticed this.

Types 2, 5 and 8 are all Rejection Types that share a feeling that they have been rejected and have therefore developed a particular pattern of rejecting others. The feeling of being the one who rejects first can ease the sense of being rejected, but the three Types each feel themselves to be rejected in different ways. For Twos, it is a matter of self-esteem and stems from the sense that they are not worthy of love or that they are re- quired to do something special in order to be loved. For Eights, it derives from the fact that they know that there is a great deal of energy within them, which sometimes expresses itself forcefully and which therefore frightens or pushes others away. As such, the Eight can often feel that they are too much for others to handle and that others cannot deal with their energy. Fives also feel rejected, but on a larger scale, in that the feel- ing derives from a sense of not really belonging, that they are too difficult to understand or be with, or are simply strange or mysterious. All three Rejection Types thus share one or other sense that others will not want them or be able to deal with them, which is precisely why they place this demand on their close relationships.

Frustration

Frustration means that, in your experience, the Figure or Figures were present, but that you did not have access to precisely what they represent. It also means that you were able to recognise that it was possible to re- ceive, for example, empathy, attention and love from the Nurturing Fig- ure, but that you did not receive what you would have liked. You therefore have a well-developed sense of what empathy, sensitivity toward others and unconditional love represent, as well as how they show themselves and are expressed, but you experienced them as fragmented during your childhood and therefore express them in a fragmented way yourself.

Types 1, 4 and 7 are Frustration Types, sharing a sense that they could easily have received a certain form of attention, but that they themselves did not. Everyone else may well have received attention – which is proof that it was indeed possible to receive it – but they themselves were never given the form of attention they needed. Ones are frustrated over a lack of clarity, order or willingness to make an effort. They have a deep sense that others ought to do things better and live up to proper standards. Frustration for Fours stems from others having (or being) precisely that which it is meaningful to have (or be). So, if others have partners, theirs will be gorgeous, while the Four's own partner will be rather dull in com- parison. However, for Fours it is at least possible to have a desirable part- ner, so they tend to want something that they believe will make them happy and which from their perspective has made others happy. The frustration of Sevens derives from things never turning out to be as they had anticipated in their plans and thoughts. Every time they imagine a wonderful evening with friends, it turns out not to be as wonderful as they had imagined.

Attachment

Attachment Types have the sense that they "suppose" they had access to what the Figure or Figures represent, but that this was not of particular interest to them, or that they simply expected it to be accessible to them. If you are an Attachment Type, you have a diffuse or ambivalent sense of what, for example, empathy, sensitivity to others and unconditional love consist of. You will be willing to offer them, although you may find it difficult to determine how to do so. The same applies to your own self-es- teem, empathy for yourself and unconditional love for yourself.

Types 3, 6 and 9 are Attachment Types: they attempt to cling on to situa- tions in which they are comfortable. Threes tend to have stable personal- ities, so they do not shift very far from their usual state. Many Threes have a strikingly stable emotional register, and it is not easy to knock them off balance emotionally. Sixes tend to desire a stable and predictable day- to- day existence, while Nines tend not to engage in activities likely to disturb their comfort. Attachment Types are flexible in their personalities, but only to the extent that this flexibility secures stability and comfort in their lives, so it can be difficult to give them feedback. However, when they grasp the point of the feedback, they rapidly accept it – almost as though it were their own idea.

The Figures and your experience of them

- The way that you related to the Nurturing or Protective Figures (rejection, frustration, attachment) *is your own personal percep- tion and thus the way YOU as a child perceived the situation as you were growing up*. This is not, therefore, necessarily a descrip- tion of the objective truth, but it was the way that you experienced things, and it was that filter or value-set through which you saw the world.
- The *Nurturing Figure* is not necessarily your mother, but the Figure that provided care, love, peace of mind, serenity, balance, nourishment and warmth – and who took you in their arms. I will expand on this topic in the chapter "About the Nurturing Figure".
- The *Protective Figure* is not necessarily your father, but the Figure that established boundaries, principles, rules and structures – and who determined the course to be taken, was consistent and embodied justice. I will expand on this topic in the chapter "About the Protective Figure".
- Everyone had a Nurturing and a Protective Figure as they grew up, even in a single-parent family. A grandfather, grandmother, uncle, aunt or a close friend might well have fulfilled either the nurturing or the protective role.
- The same figure cannot fulfil both the protective and the nurtur- ing roles.

What Object Relations are *not* about

Object Relations *only* describe your relationship with one of the Figures – they do not describe the nature of your relationship (that is, how it was experienced) with the other Figure. If, for example, you are a Type 1 and have a Frustration-relationship with the Protective Figure, Object Relations do *not* explain how you related to the Nurturing Figure.

ABOUT THE NURTURING FIGURE

The Nurturing Figure represents a range of qualities typically related to the nurturing role. These qualities can also relate to the protective role, but I have chosen to review a number of selected qualities and their deeper significance for our own personal development as well as the dy- namics of our close relationships.

We typically associate the following qualities with the Nurturing Figure:

- Love (platonic)
- Satisfaction of needs
- Value, including the ability to see yourself and others in the round; self-acceptance and self-esteem
- Openness, willingness to listen, curiosity
- Care
- Attentiveness
- Identification with honesty
- Serenity and balance
- Ability to see oneself and others in the round; self-acceptance
- Self-esteem
- Gratefulness
- Contentment

Below, I will elaborate on the following qualities with the intention of demonstrating just how important these qualities are for the way in which you perceive yourself and others:

- Love (platonic)
- Satisfaction of needs
- Value, including the ability to see yourself and others in the round; self-acceptance and self-esteem

Love (platonic)

The quality of love provides the sense that someone or something is lovable. A baby can be lovable when, as a tiny, vulnerable creature, it gazes at the world without really understanding anything at all; yet it is nonetheless a wondrous miracle. A baby that looks us in the eye demands nothing of us and receives nothing from us but our deepest love – particularly if it is our own child. We demand nothing in return, and we give our love unconditionally to this new soul, newly arrived in our world. It is also difficult for us to fully explain exactly what we feel or experience, yet we still sense that our encounter with the baby is unique and sublime. If you have children yourself, you will undoubtedly experience moments where you feel a close attachment to your child and when everything makes sense. Time and space dissolve, and you wish you could have more such miracles – or perhaps that you could extend the moment. Yet if you start thinking too much about it, the magic disappears. And if you attempt to cling on to such moments or demand that you enjoy such mo- ments all the time, things can go horribly wrong. I work with two con- cepts of love: the first I call *essential love* and the *second personified love*.

Essential love

Essential love is the love you have for yourself, for others and, yes, for life itself. It is unconditional and unprejudiced, and it originates in your acceptance of love for yourself. When you acknowledge and enter into an essential love, you also understand that you do not need others to ex- press their love for you in a special way. If, for example, others say "I love you", you are happy on their behalf that they can access such a feeling, while you also recognise that it really has nothing to do with you, but is, rather, a result of the other being able to feel love. Moreover, you feel at ease with yourself: you do not have a bad conscience about receiving love for yourself, nor do you become self-absorbed in this love for your- self. When you have access to essential love, you *are* the love.

Personified love

Personified love is the love you receive or give to others and which you experience as being either good or bad – and which you either want or do not want. You have the idea that you can decide whether you will be surrounded by love, or whether the way in which you will be in love must take a particular form. Personified love implies conditions, demands, prerequisites, comparisons and evaluations. If you generally have access to personified love, you will have forceful views about how your partner should love you, accommodate you and notice you. You will probably have many explanations as to why it is important for you that love should be shown in a specific way, and you will have a tendency to be stubborn in your account of why you ought to be loved in a specific way, as well as why this way will make you happy, satisfied or serene.

Satisfaction of needs

The quality of need satisfaction is the condition that arises when your needs are satisfied. This can refer to a need for food, drink, warmth and so forth, which are necessarily provided by those around you when you are an infant. As a baby you are not in a position to express your wants and needs, and you must work out special ways of drawing attention to the fact that you are, for example, hungry. These mechanisms still exist within you and are closely connected with feelings of security/surviv- al and well-being/enjoyment. These, then, are powerful impulses, and as you gradually build up your experience of how it feels to have your needs satisfied, your desire to have them satisfied increases. The state of *hunger* is closely connected to need satisfaction and is related to the need to hunt and to fight or to make a stand to meet your needs. There is also, however, a tendency toward dependence, whereby a positive stimulus achieved through meeting a need runs out of control, regard- less of whether this applies to, for example, alcohol, sugar, sex, drugs or caffeine. Here I work with two concepts of need satisfaction, the first of which I term *essential need satisfaction* and the second *personified need satisfaction*.

Satisfaction of essential needs

You experience an essential need satisfaction when you achieve a natu- ral balance between hunger and satiation, and when you can satisfy your needs yourself. You will experience a sense of gratefulness that you can access the "now", and although you might wish to remove yourself from the moment or make plans for the future, you will be aware of an ac- ceptance and an appreciation of what exists right here and now. You will naturally be hungry and thirsty, but you will stop eating drinking when you feel full. You will also drink coffee and alcohol, and you will know when you do not need more to drink. You will enjoy every moment of a period of erotic activity without searching for a particular highlight for yourself or your partner. The satisfaction of your essential needs sharp- ens your sense of what you need, while avoiding overconsumption and an imbalance in your consumption. Personally, it has been an uplifting experience for me to discover the freedom derived from not snacking constantly when working from home; the same applies when attending places such as retreats where one eats at fixed times.

Personified satisfaction of needs

A personified need satisfaction occurs when you routinely eat the same breakfast without giving a second thought to having an extra cup of cof- fee in the office or overlooking your hunger and fatigue all day long. You will also have a ready-made elucidation for why you eat as you do, why you require your need to be satisfied in a specific way, or why others do not satisfy your need correctly. If you generally have access to a person- alised type of need satisfaction, you will seek out erotic highlights, which must take a specific form or feeling, you will crave a morning coffee, or you will overconsume (even tending toward something resembling mis- use) sweets, tobacco, caffeine or alcohol. Personified need satisfaction is closely associated with the mouth and lips, such that intense personified need satisfaction can manifest itself by you requiring your partner to kiss you in a particular way, by calming yourself through touching your lips, or by enjoying eating in such a way that you are able to relish the full fla- vour of your food and drink.

Value, including the ability to see yourself and others in the round; self-acceptance and self-esteem

The quality of self-acceptance and self-esteem – or the ability to appreciate yourself – involves knowing your worth very specifically; that is, you can specify your human qualities minutely, as well as accepting them and cherishing them. This quality also involves being at peace with yourself and recognising that everything that you are is whole, complete, original and unique – and you are well aware that you do not need to do anything, deliver anything or present anything in order to be valued. Ba- bies have no sense of their own worth, or that they need to do anything to be valued – they are simply what they are and have no sense of whether they are valued or not. In our loving encounters with infants, we do not consider whether we are valued either: we are just inordinately happy in our encounters with the child.

Here I work with two concepts of worth. The first I call *essential value* and the second *personified value*.

Essential value

An essential value is a value such that you experience the sense that be- ing yourself is in itself valuable. To be just here and now, with precisely that which is here and now, has worth in itself. This quality is represented in all three centres. *Rationally* you have no doubt about your worth, and this does not become an unreflective or naïve evaluation of your worth. You have a deep *emotional* sense of who and what you are, and you know that it is impossible to ascribe any value to what you are, other than the fact that you are valued. And, *physically*, you recognise your value, often through your actions.

On those occasions when you really feel your worth, you will also have the feeling that you are creating something valuable for others, and you will also feel that you are becoming better and better at the things you do. One could also say that when you are at ease in your own worth, thereby gaining both an insight into and an acceptance of yourself, you will con- tribute something that others perceive to be extremely valuable. One of the reasons for this is that you look like someone that others would like to be: that is, someone who is attentive to him/herself. Given the context of very challenging coaching situations, my experience has been that the only thing the coach did was to be attentive and full of their own worth. The client was then able to reflect and gradually feel that it is possible to recognise one's own value.

Personified value

A personified value is one where you believe that you must be something distinctive, play a specific role or behave in a particular manner. You will also demand that others perform a specific role, and you will therefore be critical about the behaviour of others. Personified value is closely associated with severe internal criticism, so that an inner voice insist- ently commands you to behave in a particular way. This inner dialogue can be difficult to endure, and it therefore expresses itself as criticism of others. By the same token, you may come to feel that you are the only person behaving worthily or in the correct way. If you generally have ac- cess to personified value, it will be difficult or even impossible for your partner to do things in the way that you want, and your inner frustration will be channelled toward your partner. You will also have a tendency to rigidly persevere in fixed roles which you believe are the right ones for you – both for yourself and for those around you. You may have strong opinions about how you should carry out your role as mother, boss, col- league, partner, host and so forth, which can also result in you having fixed expectations of others in their roles as children, employees, col- leagues, partners and guests.

ABOUT THE PROTECTIVE FIGURE

The Protective Figure represents a range of qualities typically associated with the protective role. These qualities can also be related to the Nurtur- ing Figure, but I have chosen to review a range of selected qualities and their deeper significance for our own personal development, as well as for the dynamics of our close relationships.

Typically, the following qualities will be used in the protective role:

- Interpreting the world/reality correctly
- Establishing pathways
- Willpower
- Giving orders
- Ending relationships
- Proactiveness
- Sticking to principles
- Individualisation
- Courage
- Strategic thinking
- Strength
- Standing up for a cause or for oneself
- Support
- Establishing boundaries
- Taking up cudgels on behalf of causes important for one's values
- Perseverence
- Expressing opinions clearly
- Expressing wishes

Below, I will elaborate on the following qualities with the intention of demonstrating just how important these qualities are for the way in which we perceive ourselves and others.

- Interpreting the world/reality correctly
- Establishing pathways
- Willpower

Interpreting the world/reality correctly

This quality is about interpreting one's surroundings correctly. We are reminded of the result of an experiment in which the researchers de- cided to study a living cell and to remove its "intelligence", that is, the nucleus with its DNA. The researchers expected that the cell would die, but it actually continued to thrive in the best of health, although obvi- ously unable to reproduce as a result of its missing DNA. The researchers discovered that the cell's real "intelligence" is to be found in its mem- brane, the purpose of which is to interpret the world correctly and then to report to the cell about modifying its energy usage, moving, attacking invading viruses and so forth. This means that all living cells in our body constantly attempt to read and interpret the outside world and then to signal what the correct action is right now. This quality also includes ob- jectivity, the capacity to prioritise and to be consistent, thus filtering out misconceptions and assumptions that could otherwise blur a picture of the outside world.

Essential interpretation

An essential interpretation is one in which you have a clear sense of what is happening around you, and it also involves an acceptance of the cir- cumstances that obtain in your life. This does not mean that you blindly accept all conditions that you create yourself or that others put in place, given that an essential interpretation also challenges and sees through habitual thinking or futile dogmas. When you express an essential inter- pretation, you will experience a feeling that things are simple: although these may well be sorrowful or painful, you are capable of encountering sorrow without attempting to change things. When, for example, your reading of a situation is such that you are in a position to feel grief on behalf of someone you care about, you are capable of feeling this grief without feeling the need to change the situation for the other, and you do not try to change reality for others: you do not try to fix their problems or make it easier for them to be in a state of grief. An essential interpretation gives you the possibility of moving easily through life and not being hin- dered or detained by attempting to alter reality or change others so that it is easier to be you. Particularly if you are working to realise your calling or passion, you will be well aware that the path is full of obstacles and frustration, but because you also optimally interpret the path (which is, after all, part of reality), you will have the greater acceptance necessary to realise your calling and to overcome natural obstacles.

Personified interpretation

A personified interpretation is one in which you see reality through a filter. This filter requires you to see certain elements of reality and to eliminate others. You might have a filter making you aware of what oth- ers think of you, and you will therefore read those signals that relate to their perception of you, while completely ignoring your own perception of yourself. Or you might have a filter so that you are conscious of doing things properly and correctly, and you will therefore interpret the signals suggesting good/bad, right/wrong, true/false and so forth, whilst com- pletely forgetting the many nuances that also characterise our existence. If you generally access a personified interpretation, you will seek out par- ticular failings in your partner and have a tendency to regard your part- ner as a development project, to be constantly improved and developed further. It can appear that you are dissatisfied with how your partner is, and that you wish your partner to be someone else…who conforms to the filter through which you see the world.

Establishing pathways

This quality relates to establishing a course for one's own life and there- by detaching oneself from the course indicated or stipulated by family, culture and the wider world. It also entails detachment and individualisation; in my experience, when extremely talented people at some point detach themselves from their teacher/master, this action requires them to be able to stand on their own two feet and find their own voice, rather than simply repeating the words of their teacher/master. When we es- tablish a pathway, it is hardly a conscious action, but often a feeling that we have to get somewhere in the world – not necessarily with a particular reward in mind, but more with a sense of "Just because...I can't not do this". The more you follow your own direction, the more you will leave behind what you know, what you are safe with.

Essential pathway

The essential pathway is the pathway in which you are both in flow with what you are doing while also feeling that you are heading in the right di- rection. This feels like listening to a call that is crucial for you and which is bruising for you, yet also enables you to create many values for your- self and those around you. I work with the idea that we are born with a special human gift, which we are almost obliged to put to good use, and which we should strive to pass on to others around us and the next gen- eration. Thus, when you take your essential pathway, you will bring both your personal and human gifts into play, also enabling others to model them and integrate them into their own lives.

Personified pathway

The personified pathway is one in which you believe that you must get to a certain place in your life, achieve something specific, or be a particular person or role. Perhaps you believe that this is about being the best at school or work, or the best at whatever you are doing. Or it might be that you believe you must act in a certain way in your role as parent, leader, coach or pupil – and that this particular way of being will lead you to the place you want to be. If you are particularly absorbed in a personi- fied pathway, you will have a tendency to act on the basis of fear rather than love; that is, you will do things out of fear of what will happen if you do not do them. It may be that you believe that you ought to be at a workplace for a certain period of time because otherwise your CV would not look so impressive. The consequence of this would be that you move along a pathway that is constructed on the basis of a fear of potential consequences rather than a love of your work.

Willpower

This quality relates to a willingness to give up something to achieve something. Many other qualities are associated with this quality, includ- ing an ability to stand up for a cause (or yourself), to struggle when nec- essary, to endure the blows when they come your way, and to accept the consequences of your decisions. Your willpower can naturally appear stubborn or obdurate if you forget that your willpower is also associated with gentleness and a combination of strength and flexibility. You will also acquire a sense of indomitability when you connect with your will, and you will establish followers on the basis of your determination to make things happen. When you possess willpower, you will fight to the death for a cause, in a way reminiscent of the concept of *irimi*, derived from Japanese martial arts: this involves attacking directly, or initiating an attack oneself. Most leaders must acquire this quality of willpower and the ability to fight for a cause with "life and honour", and if a leader does not have willpower, it can be difficult to master the art of leadership on the basis of professional skills alone.

Wikipedia: In Japanese martial arts, irimi (入り身) is the act of enter- ing straight into a technique, as opposed to the more indirect entrance into technique called tenkan. In basic training, irimi usually looks like a step forward, straight or at an angle but usually ending with the body facing the attacker, rather than in the direction of the step. To enter with irimi, the defender needs to move in the very moment of the attack or even him- self initiate it.

Essential willpower

Essential willpower is that willpower in which you have a deep-rooted contact with what is important for you. You have established a relation- ship with yourself and those around you, and you are capable of issuing orders, ending relationships and being a ruthless negotiator. This type of willpower is not a simple instrument for getting things to be as you want them to be, and it is not characterised by inappropriate discrimination, exercise of power or domination of others in order to get your way. When you are aware of your essential willpower, you will often smile about how simple it is, and how easy it is to give up those things that prevent you from exercising your will. You will discover a natural quality of en- durance, ensuring that you go the whole way and do not give up when things seem difficult and occasionally contradictory. Willpower removes the frustration associated with the dilemmas that often arise in the space between wishes and obligations, as you will be capable of easily distin- guishing between gratifying your desires and fulfilling those tasks that are obligatory in their nature.

Personified willpower

Personified willpower is the willpower that is exercised when you need to secure agreement or to get your way. This is associated with a form of reward (your "just deserts") and can arise when you have worked hard and think that you deserve a break, a cup of coffee or the recognition of others. Such willpower expresses itself in the form of a demand but is experienced as something you want or should reasonably have. Person- ified willpower often becomes stubbornness or conceitedness with re- gard to something you perceive as your just deserts for some hard work you have carried out. If you stick rigidly to your personified willpower, you will begin to feel that you have certain rights in your close relation- ships and that you will lose something of yourself if you do not feel the energy that comes from exercising your willpower.

THE NURTURING AND PROTECTIVE QUALITIES: CONCLUDING REMARKS

In the preceding review, the nurturing and protective qualities naturally overlap to some extent, and there can be plenty of love within the protective qualities and plenty of willpower in the nurturing qualities. The above review primarily serves the purpose of providing you with a sense of how we can be in balance or imbalance with these qualities and how imbalance can often seem disturbing or even occasionally destructive in our close relationships. When you begin to work at balancing the qual- ities, your close relationships are an obvious place to start practising – particularly if both partners are willing to practise and know that prac- tice makes perfect.

OBJECT RELATIONS FOR THE NINE ENNEAGRAM TYPES

Why are Object Relations so important in close relationships? This chap- ter is about relationships between the Types, and here Object Relations also play a role. The reason for this is that the whole theory behind the Object Relations revolves around how we mirrored ourselves in the Pro- tective and/or Nurturing Figure(s) during our early years – and thus how we have mirrored ourselves in those people who have been of critical importance in and for our lives. We repeat this mirroring in our close relationships and build up expectations of our partner about delivering (or partially delivering) some of what we did not receive (or only partially received) from our parents or the significant adults in our childhood.

The Object Relation for Type 1

Type 1 has a Frustration-relationship with the Protective Figure such that, while the Figure was in fact capable of fulfilling the role by putting in place clear and consistent pathways, it did not actually do so. It is worth noting in this context that the frustration arises because the Figure was not consistent and therefore did not always, indisputably, without interruption and without error, indicate the qualities embodied in the Protective Figure.

At an early stage, the Type 1 fully understood that it is in fact possi- ble to demonstrate the qualities of the Protective Figure, as many (if not all) of these qualities were often (if not always) presented to the young Type 1. At the same time, a sense of having a direction in life is inherent in the protective qualities, and this sense later appears as a mission or cause that is more important than much else in the One's existence. As an adult, the Type 1 perceives that there is a higher cause to fight for – or indeed to live for – and this cause is often more important than the Type 1 him/herself and his/her relationships.

The young One thus encounters an inconsistent set of protective guidelines in the external world and therefore begins to construct un-ambiguous, consistent, perfect and flawless protective guidelines in his/ her internal world. These start out as mental structures and then, over time, become emotional and physical structures. This means that feel- ings such as frustration, disempowerment, bitterness and resentment are generated, and the body begins to form structures such that the One becomes awkward, explosive and obstinate in his/her expression.

Close relationships

In close relationships – regardless of the other's Type – the One has a natural frustration over the other's way of exhibiting protective qualities.

This arises because the One judges or prejudges the other's approach to, for example, cleaning, timekeeping, eating or maintaining their emo- tional and physical health.

Close relationships: key points to bear in mind

- When and how do you make demands on your partner?
- How do you attempt to get your partner to follow your rules?
- Which principles should your partner buy into?
- What are the consequences if your partner does not buy into your principles?

The Object Relation in all of us

A frustrated relationship with the Protective Figure resides within all of us and is an expression of the fact that we want others to live up to our own high standards, that we often judge others for being wrong or because they should be different, and that we can judge ourselves too harshly if we have made a mistake.

Instincts

Our Instincts also have a considerable influence on the dynamics of our close relationships. There follows a brief description of the three In- stincts characterising the Type 1, as well as a short guide to a number of key points to bear in mind regarding this Type.

Self-preservation – tendencies

- Tendency toward anxiety around financial well-being and physi- cal health
- Attachment of significance to cleanliness, aesthetics, good order and hygiene (own and other people's)
- Strict control by the superego over both work and pleasure
- Projection of blame onto the outside world if cleaning is not done properly, not enough money saved up, or diet not maintained
- All-or-nothing behaviour (unhealthy)

If you identify with Type 1, this Instinct, in conjunction with the Object Relation, makes you stricter and sharper in your attitudes toward your partner. You have a tendency to compel your partner to follow your principles within the relationship and at home, and you have a tendency to experience a breakdown in the relationship when your partner does not follow your principles around, for example, health and cleaning.

Self-preservation – points to bear in mind
- Bear in mind that you make demands on your partner that do not necessarily conform to the way that they want to live their lives
- Bear in mind that you can make unreasonable demands on your- self. It can be sensible to carry out a detailed examination of what it is reasonable to demand of yourself
- Bear in mind how you can physically relax more, so that you can prevent bodily wear and tear

Social – tendencies
- Focus intently on ethical and moral issues in society as well as the norms associated with good practice or processes keeping society on track
- Would patiently invest substantial resources in creating the right frameworks in society for young people – those in need and those whom we ought to help
- Strong beliefs and opinions. These can become extreme in the One's role as, for example, politician, police officer, judge, priest, head teacher
- Tendency to anxiety over human imperfection

If you relate to Type 1, this Instinct, in conjunction with the Object Relation, gives you a greater focus on connections outside your relationship, and you will have a tendency to absorb yourself more in your role as, for example, police officer, judge, priest, or head teacher. You will, furthermore, tend to demand that your partner supports you in your cause and, as a minimum, gives you the time and space to engage in your cause.

Social – points to bear in mind

- Bear in mind how your deep engagement with "society" can deprive you of your "freedom" – and bear in mind how your inner dialogue begins to explain why it is important for you to engage so deeply!
- Bear in mind how sharp and prickly you can be in your attitudes (even if you do not express these verbally), and thereby how quickly you can lose your rapport with those around you
- Bear in mind that you can come to appear as arrogant and condescending when you "fight" for your cause

Sexual – tendencies

- Tendency to pressurise those in close relationships to also live up to his/her high standards of what it is to be a good person
- Can feel betrayed if someone in a close relationship behaves "wrongly" in the relationship
- Seeks the perfect partner without flaws, who also shares the same ideals with regard to relationships, finances, sex, children etc.
- Would like to be able to confirm, and approve of, what his/her partner is doing
- Is convinced that (s)he has worked hard to prepare for the "right one" – and will therefore feel betrayed and lonely if the "right one" does not turn up

If you relate to Type 1, this Instinct, in conjunction with the Object Relation, will produce in you extremely high principles in relation to what constitutes a "proper" lover, and you might therefore find it difficult to find a partner who lives up to your demands and principles for a "prop- er" lover. When you have found a partner, you will tend to be suspicious about whether (s)he can consistently live up to your requirements in a "proper" partner.

Sexual – points to bear in mind

- Bear in mind that you (sometimes) make unreasonable demands of your future or current partner
- Bear in mind how quickly you judge others and construct a narrative around your belief that if only they tried harder or listened to you more, all would be well
- Bear in mind that your collaborator or colleague is trying to share their knowledge, experience and wisdom with you – but that you have a tendency to shut down if their perspective does not match your conception of the world

The Object Relation for Type 2

Type 2 has a Rejection-relationship with the Protective Figure, which means that the Protective Figure has not been present; therefore the Two has not been able to access the Protective Figure's qualities to mirror him/herself in. Not being able to project ourselves in certain qualities has the consequence that we do not learn to master them in our early years. The result of this is that the Two typically finds it dif- ficult to express or demonstrate the protective qualities – particularly in expressing clear wishes or refusing requests. Young Type 2s focus exclusively on the nurturing qualities and therefore become masters of the qualities embodied in the Nurturing Figure. As adults, Type 2s begin to create relationships in which they are "the source of love" for the other, and they want to construct close ties with the people that are important in the life of the Type 2. There can be a tendency for Twos to forget themselves and their own needs, and it can be difficult for them to recognise their own needs – and therefore to articulate these needs to those close to them. The Type 2 often wishes that those close to them would (or should) recognise the Two's wants and take it upon themselves to provide them to the Two. The young Two thus experi- ences being the "source of love" as of great value and therefore begins to cultivate a vulnerability and attentiveness to others' state of mind, developing a special feeling for the needs of others (or whatever is nec- essary to re-establish their good mood). Over time, the Two develops a considerable emotional capacity, which often finds its bodily or phys- ical expression in the form of actively doing something for others. This activism on behalf of others is a type of confirmation that the relation- ship is real and that it is meaningful, while physical activity is evidence that the Two contributes positively to the relationship.

Close relationships

In a close relationship – regardless of the other's Type – the Two needs to feel secure in the relationship and will go the extra mile to ensure that it succeeds. At the same time, it is a requirement that the other be grateful for the Two's considerable efforts on behalf of the relationship. Moreo- ver, a need gradually emerges requiring the other to take up the role as the relationship's Protective Figure, upon whom the Two can lean or to whom the Two can transfer some of the considerable responsibilities the Two has taken upon him/herself throughout his/her whole life.

Points to bear in mind in close relationships

- How does it look when you sacrifice yourself in your relationship, and is the fact that it is you that sacrifices yourself in harmony with your partner's position?
- What is it that is difficult when your partner expresses what the Protective Figure stands for (refusal, saying "no", expressing their views about you clearly etc.)?
- What do you expect to achieve when you punish your partner by shutting down the relationship?

The Object Relation in all of us

The Rejection-relationship with the Protective Figure exists in all of us and expresses itself through the fact that it can be difficult to accept re- fusals from (or to say "no" to) those we care about, while we can also be in doubt whether others care about us, or if we are not contributing anything to the relationship, and we all need to be noticed, heard and accommodated. Finally, it can be difficult for many of us to express our wishes to others, often because we ourselves do not recognise our own needs.

Instincts

Our Instincts also have a significant influence upon the dynamics of our close relationships. There follows a brief description of the three Instincts for Type 2 and a short guide to a number of points to bear in mind for this Type.

Self-preservation – tendencies
- A general need to be seen is magnified by taking over the self-preserving responsibilities of others
- A tendency to care for yourself by caring for others – enjoying your own party is not permitted
- Sacrificing your own self-preserving tendencies: this makes you meaningful
- Tendency to martyrdom or overdramatisation of illness

If you relate to Type 2, these Instincts, in conjunction with the Object Relation, will produce in you greater self-sacrifice concerning the more physical aspects of the relationship, which can result in you giving your partner time and space to train, but also in forgetting to train yourself. You will also have a tendency to overdramatise things when you are ill, because you tend to feel that you are always there for your partner and that now your partner must be there for you. You feel extremely let down if your partner refuses to fetch your medicine when you are sick, as a "no" is regarded as a "no" to the entire relationship.

Self-preservation – points to bear in mind
- Bear in mind that you have a tendency to ignore your own health (training, sleep, healthy diet etc.)
- Bear in mind that you overdramatise how difficult it is for you to alter, for example, a habit or lifestyle. By reaching out for help, everything becomes much easier
- Be aware that when you become irritated with others, this is often because you are irritated with yourself for having "sacrificed" yourself

Social – tendencies
- Tendency to cultivate an extensive social network and to have a

large number of active social relationships

- Speaking to strangers as though they have been friends for many years, and finding it easy to make people feel welcome
- Seeking acknowledgement from the most significant people in a social network, and looking for evidence of this acknowledgement
- Happy to help important people with good advice and guidance about achieving a better life – particularly regarding relationships
- May build relationships by sharing "confidential" information

If you relate to Type 2, these Instincts, in conjunction with your Object Relation, will make you more outgoing, and your partner might misunderstand the positive, welcoming and friendly signals you send to others. You will have a greater focus on your network and social relationships in your professional life than on the close relationship itself, and you will require your partner not to place limits on your activities. Your desire to be "mother" or "father" to those outside your close relationship is sometimes puzzling for your partner, and you will encounter difficulties in allocating your attention (love) equally to everyone in your external relationships and the one/those in your closer relationship(s).

Social – points to bear in mind

- Bear in mind that you can end up playing your relationships off against each other by, for example, sharing confidential information
- Bear in mind that you can tire yourself out by believing that you have to maintain, and be important for, a large group of people
- Bear in mind that not everyone desires particularly intimate or close moments

Sexual – tendencies

- See yourself as *the* close relation, *the* real friend others can ring
- Tendency to need to win a friend/partner/colleague over to your side – victory is secured through targeted focus/attentiveness and "flattery"

- Enjoy talking about "relationships" with those in relationships with you
- Enjoy having several groups of friends, each of which is able to deliver what you want
- A tendency to explain how "real" love feels – particularly to those who cannot feel it
- Seductive attentiveness and exaggerated charm

If you relate to Type 2, this Instinct, in conjunction with your Object Relation, will make you extremely intense and seductive. Your partner will feel flattered and engaged – and feel that (s)he is noticed, heard and accommodated. You will tend to have a kind of suspicion about whether the relationship is real, whether love is true, whether you can fundamen- tally trust your partner and thus whether love has really arrived in your life. You may therefore have a tendency to test your partner's love, and, because you have your own idea of how a true relationship and true love ought to be experienced, these tests can exhaust your partner. This can be expressed as rejections or withdrawals from your partner, which will, in turn, lead you to feel that love has not, after all, arrived in your life.

Sexual – points to bear in mind

- Bear in mind that you can overextend yourself in your closest relationships
- Bear in mind that you can appear rather saccharine when you try to win people over through flattery – and this is not positive for everyone
- Bear in mind that you should learn how to be alone – without being lonely

The Object Relation for Type 3

Type 3 has an Attachment-relationship with the Nurturing Figure, with the result that there is a diffuse relationship with the nurturing qualities. This created an uncertain sense of the nurturing qualities in the young Three, so that they did not take a clear position on whether there was love or care in their life, although there probably was in one form or oth- er. At the same time, it is in this area that the Three has been most chal- lenged in life, usually leading to a diffuse or insecure relationship with him/herself.

Type 3s have often circled around the great existential questions, but tended to take a somewhat superficial approach to questions such as what is the meaning of life, what should I devote myself to, why am I lonely, and so forth. By "superficial" I mean that the Three wanted quick answers to questions, so darker feelings around such topics did not de- tain them for too long. As a rule, later in life, these questions become central in the life of the Three, who now seeks meaning in a clear, meas- urable form. Many Threes want to find an area in which they can cre- ate meaning, experience something meaningful, or acquire a quality or qualification that is worthwhile. One might say that their diffuse internal relationship with themselves creates a desire to have a clear relationship with "something" in the external world.

The young Three experiences the feeling of being skilled or having mastery over an area and that this mastery has a purpose or creates meaning. Gradually, a personality is constructed around these endeav- ours and activities, and many Threes sense that they are more rational and action-oriented than emotional. Planning and working things out from start to finish – combined with projects and activities – become clear patterns in the lives of Threes, who are frequently so steadfast that they rarely come into contact with their feelings or their inner universe.

Close relationships

In close relationships – regardless of the other's Type – the Three has a need to be proud of their partner, and their partner must be able to match the high tempo of the Three. Threes also need a form of recogni- tion in their close relationships; moreover, they have a tendency to fix the other's problems rather than listening to what the other has to say.

Points to bear in mind in close relationships

- When do you start forgetting to listen to your partner and instead start fixing your partner's "problems"?
- When do you operate alone rather than including everyone?
- When do you think that mind-reading is possible, and what is your reaction to your partner not perceiving things as you do?
- What form of recognition do you want from your partner, and what are the consequences if you do not receive it?

The Object Relation in all of us

The Attachment-relationship with the Nurturing Figure exists in all of us and finds its expression in the fact that it can be difficult to know which role we ought to play in life, whether there is a role for us, and indeed whether we should play a role at all…or simply be ourselves.

Instincts

Our Instincts also have a significant influence on the dynamics of our close relationships. There follows a brief description of the three Instincts characterising Type 3, along with a short guide to a range of points to bear in mind for the Type.

Self-preservation – tendencies

- Work to build conspicuous security and material goods. Security derives from saving, property, insured art etc.
- Fine-tune their efficiency, enabling them to build as much securi- ty as possible; fear illness

- Recognition is derived from their "secure platform" and tangible results such as pay rises
- Extremely optimistic with regard to time
- A tendency to test time limits and expectations too far – and thereby risk burning out

If you relate to Type 3, these Instincts, in conjunction with the Object Relation, make you hard-working – almost a workaholic. If you live in the western world, you will be focussed on money and work hard to en- sure you have money for yourself and your family, so that you and your family can make use of as many of life's opportunities as possible. Your family will tend to become a project, and you will expect your partner to understand why you work so hard – for yourself and your family. You will demand to be noticed, heard and to have your needs accommodated, to such a degree that you will perceive it as a criticism if your partner com- ments on your diligence. Your Object Relation also produces a tendency for you to believe that mind-reading is possible and that your partner should be able to appreciate the background for your many activities – and thus ought not to complain about you working so much.

Self-preservation – points to bear in mind
- Bear in mind that you can focus too much on "money" or another type of "value", which can be measured and weighed and which symbolises your success
- Bear in mind that you are extremely optimistic with regard to time, such that there is a danger of burnout or poor quality of life
- Bear in mind that you can focus so intently on your practical tasks that you lose your relationships

Social – tendencies
- Recognition comes from your social environment and is meas- ured in terms of being valued within this culture and current trends
- An extreme networker and name-dropper; visible on social media

- Seeking out the appropriate position in every social context in which you find yourself
- A tendency to show off achievements; great weight placed on having the right social identity

If you relate to Type 3, these Instincts, in conjunction with your Object Relation, lead you to focus outside your relationship, and there will be a tendency for your partner to end up as an accessory in your successful life. The love that you seek, with your foundation in the Object Relation, you find outside your relationship, within your work, projects and tasks. If this focus on external circumstances becomes unbalanced, your part- ner will start to complain, prompting you to think that you are not loved or cared for. Your partner's complaints are perceived as criticism of you as a person, and, given that your Object Relation gives you an idea that mind-reading is possible, you will question why your partner cannot un- derstand why it is important for you to "show off" your fabulous holidays together on social media.

Social – points to bear in mind
- Bear in mind that you focus so much on being visible that the outside world loses interest in you – such that you become invisible or uninteresting
- Bear in mind that you focus on external success; but there is also an inner success and longing that needs to be maintained or brought to fruition
- Bear in mind that you have a tendency to overlook challenges or difficult situations and can thereby lose your grip on the real world

Sexual – tendencies
- Use intimacy to achieve attractiveness and gain recognition
- Role model for their gender (beauty, sport, health etc.)
- A representative for their partner to their partner's network
- Attract the opposite sex and have difficulty being in a relationship

and building deep emotional attachments
- Tendency to exhibitionism – an "alluring image"

If you relate to Type 3, this Instinct, in conjunction with your Object Relation, will equip you with very high ideals regarding what it is to be a "man" or a "woman". You will probably cultivate the ideal of your sex and expect your partner to do the same. With this Object Relation, you will have an extraordinarily powerful need for your partner to notice and listen to you and accommodate you in accordance with the way that you imagine yourself to be. This need is rather challenging, in that it can be difficult for your partner to fully understand what it is that you imagine yourself to be. This can mean that you feel as though you are being criti- cised because your partner fails to notice that you keep yourself in shape by training, that you follow the Italian fashion shows, or that you are in- terested in taking hiking trips in Normandy.

Sexual – points to bear in mind
- Bear in mind that you have a tendency to train or to take your interest in what it is to be "man" or "woman" to extremes. This can take the form of physical training, your diet, your clothing etc.
- Bear in mind that you can come across as being too "smart, attractive, charming, divine…" This can frighten off some people from entering into relationships or collaborations with you
- Be aware that you can listen even more to your heart and your intuition when you have to make big decisions

The Object Relation for Type 4

Type 4 has a Frustration-relationship with both Figures, meaning that the Figures were in a position to provide the protective and nurturing qualities, but that they were not provided with clarity and consistency. The result was that the Four experienced both Figures as being in a posi- tion to provide or demonstrate their qualities, but that these were not in fact provided or demonstrated to the Four in the way that the Four would have experienced as perfect.

The Type 4 develops an early and deep sense that it is possible to ac- cess contact with, and to be touched by, the sum of the qualities rep- resented by both Figures. This fully developed sense, feeling or experi- ence has, over time, become a longing for a deeply meaningful life, full of worth. It also becomes a search for the essential, the original and the unique in our existence – and a quest for the perfect, which the Four   is typically convinced can be found in one form or another within the world, whether it be in art, relationships, the spiritual, or the cultural.

The young Four does not get the feeling that their quest for the com- plete has been sanctioned, and many Fours feel that they are not no- ticed, heard or understood by their parents and siblings. This lonesome pathway early in life is gradually extended with internal fantasies and emotional journeys. There may well be a great deal of purposeful ac- tion and activity behind the internal journeys, but the rational distinc- tion between things is quickly experienced as a limitation and a factor that demystifies the fantasies and sucks some of the life out of them. For this reason, the rational is often characterised as something "negative", deathly, lifeless and lacklustre.

Close relationships

In close relationships – regardless of the other's Type – the Four has a natural frustration over all the ways that they relate to their partner. As this frustration originally took root in both Figures, it will also be the qualities from both Figures that frustrate the Four in relation to their partner. In practice, this means that the partner can generally do nothing whatsoev- er right for the Four.

Points to bear in mind in close relationships

- What is your frustration with your partner about? How does this frustration reflect a frustration within yourself?
- What are the problems that remain with you when you change (or dream of changing) your partner?
- What is it you want your partner to see in you and what do you do to ensure that your partner does see precisely this?
- What is it you hope to achieve by challenging your partner?

The Object Relation in all of us

The frustrated relationship with both Figures resides in all of us and is expressed in our deep sense that there exists a direction in life that will be worth discovering or working out, alongside a deep sense that we are connected to ourselves and something valuable, which is our self, or a particular part of our self. And these deep feelings create a longing in all of us to create a meaningful life and to be content with our own life or to mean something in the world.

Instincts

Our Instincts also have a significant influence on the dynamics of our close relationships. There follows a brief description of the three Instincts characterising Type 4, along with a short guide to a range of points to bear in mind for the Type.

Self-preservation – tendencies

- A tendency toward nest-building using objects that embody beau- ty and aesthetics – practically and materialistically

- Seeks out material objects that reinforce their mood, with a tendency toward luxury or overconsumption
- Tendency to be pernickety about physical surroundings
- A lack of stimulation or compensation from material objects can lead to self-neglect, resembling a lack of self-esteem

If you relate to Type 4, these Instincts, in conjunction with your Object Relation, make you more physically oriented, meaning that you require physical space for you to arrange and express yourself – and thereby create the right energy. You will require your partner both to give you space and to take an interest in the things that you bring with you into the physical space. It may be that you create things yourself by, for ex- ample, painting or drawing; it might be that you bring in branches or feathers from the woods, or perhaps you purchase unique French treas- ures, or discover special objects in Moroccan flea markets. Your Object Relation will, however, create an ongoing frustration that the things that are moved into (for example) your apartment never really generate the perfect energy or atmosphere, the result of which is that your frustration will be channelled towards your partner.

Self-preservation – points to bear in mind
- Bear in mind that you can exaggerate the extent to which you can furnish your physical space, and you can be locked into your idea about how your surroundings look
- Bear in mind that you have a tendency to experience "pleasure" when you are distracted, tired or under pressure. Take a walk instead!
- Bear in mind that you often "disappear" when the going gets tough. It is difficult to solve all the mysteries of life yourself. Reach out and make use of those in your close relationships.

Social – tendencies
- Need for the social environment to give expression to their eccentricity or their self-created image of being different

- Want to fit into the group, but doubt whether they belong – or whether they actually want to belong
- Tendency to feel more "at home" with others who also consider themselves outsiders
- Can find it difficult to retain jobs and will therefore need a strong, but smaller and closer, personal network to sustain them through the practical aspects of working life
- The most image-focused of Fours: an alternative lifestyle and ambitious

If you relate to Type 4, these Instincts, in conjunction with your Object Relation, will divert your attention away from your close relationship, so that you will use your surroundings or external relationships as the zone where you can express yourself. You will probably meet others who also wish to express themselves, and you may play music, work in theatre or with another art form that attracts an audience. Your partner must, of course, love what you do and have a deep insight into the importance of your art and thereby also a deep insight into you as a person; if this is not articulated by your partner, it will increase your frustration and become a condition for your being able to flourish together. As your Object Rela- tion is doubly frustrated (that is, in relation to both Figures), your ability to accept the understanding and attention you desire from your partner will be limited to the point of impossibility.

Social – points to bear in mind
- Bear in mind that you are extremely demanding about how, for example, an employer should deal with you. Purely in terms of your working life, greater flexibility could take you further
- Bear in mind that you have a tendency to evaluate or judge your-self very harshly – unrealistically so. Be more realistic with regard to the demands you make of yourself
- Bear in mind that you frequently cling rigidly to your feelings. Sometimes, it is not necessary to listen to or understand your feel-

ings; it could be better to take a walk and distance yourself from the situation

Sexual – tendencies
- On a mission to be found or saved from this world, in which one is neither noticed nor understood
- Cultivate their romantic fantasies – either with their partner directly or by simply expressing them in a more artistic way
- A tendency toward, on the one hand, vulnerability and tenderness, and, on the other, dynamic and aggressive behaviour
- Seek recognition by being able to do that something special that attracts the admiration of others, or by producing something impressive, thereby making them more desirable
- Can find themselves envying their partner for the qualities they wish they possessed themselves

If you relate to Type 4, these Instincts, in conjunction with your Object Relation, will make you intense, direct, demanding and vulnerable. You will have a tendency to fantasise about the right partner, but at a level such that it may well be difficult to meet that kind of person. You perhaps dream about a partner who has studied Eastern philosophy with indige- nous and Danish sustainable farming practices at Sydney University, has adopted twins from a family whose parents perished in an Italian earth- quake, and who lives in a collective on Møn. The frustration that is ex- pressed in your Object Relation stems from a missing sense of the quali- ties from both Figures, which means that your partner will be difficult to find, while, if you do find a partner, there will be a constant pressure on this person to remain exciting and different. On top of all that, you may mistrust or feel jealousy toward your partner if the latter becomes too exciting or attractive or shares his/her exciting aspects with others.

Sexual – points to bear in mind
- Bear in mind that you can over-romanticise and overdramatise your romantic relationships

- Bear in mind that you have a tendency to envy others and what they have, or seek what you perceive in others and lack yourself. This longing for what is "missing" can be extremely frustrating for those around you to deal with
- Bear in mind that you can train yourself to "be with" your powerful feelings rather than living them out

The Object Relation for Type 5

Type 5 has a Rejection-relationship with both the Protective and the Nurturing Figure, which means that the Five's experience was that the protective and the nurturing qualities were not present in early child- hood; they were not therefore available for the Five to mirror him/herself in and, as such, the Five did not integrate them into traditional patterns of behaviour.

Type 5 has attempted to compensate for this deficiency by trying to understand what the qualities of willpower, stamina, courage, love, care and empathy actually are. A clinical or scientific approach to these qual- ities will be a tendency we often detect in a Five. A certain objectivity will characterise the adult Five, particularly in close relationships, in which their external gestures will rarely reveal how they are feeling, in which they will seldom speak of their feelings, and in which they will not often share anything of their inner selves.

The young Five experiences a non-existent or neutral expression of these qualities and thus lacks a space to approach life's big questions such as "What happens to grandma when she dies?" or "Who has all the right answers to difficult questions?" This lack of space to go to in order to find answers appears like an abyss that begins gradually to coalesce into the Five's frequent sense of the meaninglessness of life. The young Five be- gins to express their existential horror at discovering this meaninglessness by frightening themselves and others with fantasies, drawings or stories – forms of expression that begin as rational actions, but which also have the creation of feelings and bodily sensations as their objective.

Close relationships

In close relationships – regardless of the other's Type – the Five has a nat- ural disconnection from or naturally rejects his/her partner and can be comfortable in their own company without his/her partner. I have heard of children and youngsters who wanted their parents to sit with them and watch as they played computer games. The parents should not do anything or say anything – just be with them. I also see this behaviour with adults who really just want to be together in the living room.

Points to bear in mind in close relationships

- What goes on in your head when you are staring at people (including your partner)? Are you in the process of thinking, working something out, or simply in your own world?
- When you feel like stopping everything and taking off on your own, what is the issue, and how do you include your partner in your considerations as to why, for example, you need to take a walk alone?
- Why do you feel violated when your partner wishes to hear what you feel, what is going on in your head, or wants to know whether you are OK?
- How can you function in your relationship with your partner while also sharing your thoughts about the meaning of life, the structure of the universe or the reason that you should restructure your loans?

The Object Relation in all of us

The Rejection-relation toward both Figures exists in all of us and is expressed in our sometimes really just wanting to be ourselves in our own company and simply blocking out the surrounding world. Time alone with ourselves, when nobody will know how we are, what we feel or what we are think about other people, is completely natural for all of us, and it is a quality that can help us to recharge our batteries and assist us in rediscovering meaning in the world.

Instincts

Our Instincts also have a significant influence on the dynamics of our close relationships. There follows a brief description of the three Instincts characterising Type 5, along with a short guide to a range of points to bear in mind for the Type.

Self-preservation– tendencies

- Isolation is preferable at work and in the private space – which can become a sanctum
- Energy is built up in order to meet the world in the private space
- Friendly and talkative, but exhausted by people
- Tendency to pare down the physical need for food, clothing, heat- ing etc. and can hide away from the world
- Will ensure that they do not particularly need others and can thus sustain their "absence" from the world
- As a rule, emotionally reserved and closed

If you relate to Type 5, these Instincts will, in conjunction with your Object Relation, make you more introverted and frugal. You will not have a great need for interaction with others, including your partner. It will be easy for you to be alone…and you may not notice that your partner has left you. The double rejection of both Figures means that your need for the qualities represented by both Figures is placed on the backburner, while you also want your partner to respect that you are not assailed by personal questions or needs.

Self-preservation – points to bear in mind

- Bear in mind that you have a tendency to withdraw or completely disappear physically – to the great concern of those around you. If you need time alone, share this fact with those close to you
- Bear in mind that you can also withdraw from the real world by avoiding emotions and feelings. By combining thoughts, emotions and feelings you will experience a far more nuanced truth
- Bear in mind that you can be "forgotten" by those around you, and you might therefore find it difficult to get help when you real- ly need it

Social – tendencies

- Find groups of like-minded people with whom they can share their expertise – and be specialists in their area
- Tendency to be social by means of discussions and debates about topics that make a difference – not fans of light-hearted small talk
- May well hold radical views about humanity – of which, after all, they are not a part – which they can regard with highly scornful prejudices
- Can be ambitious with regard to joining the elite

If you relate to Type 5, these Instincts will, in conjunction with your Object Relation, lead to a greater focus on the external world, and you will stimulate the qualities of both Figures by being "out" in the world. You do not necessarily have a great need for a partner, but any partner you do have you want to be a positive witness to your projects. You will enjoy debating, and in your close relationships these debates should deal with important issues. It will, however, be difficult for your partner to follow them, and this can be interpreted as meaning that your partner does not want you. Such over-interpretation can result in misunderstandings, leading you to withdraw from and/or break up the relationship.

Social – points to bear in mind

- Bear in mind that you regard yourself as "extremely knowledgeable" within your field. This means that you can seem arrogant and scornful when you are collaborating with others
- Bear in mind that your way of expressing yourself is extremely verbose, deep, nuanced, specialised, objective, technical, professional and knowledgeable – and it is the sender of the message that is responsible for ensuring that its recipient interprets it correctly
- Bear in mind that you can build relationships in ways other than sharing your knowledge – and that others care about you because you are what you are, and not because you know all there is to know about German football, The Beatles or World War Two

Sexual – tendencies

- Conflict between a lack of attachment and a desire for intense contact
- Seek a mate who can handle their self-diagnosed eccentricity
- Experimental in their close relationships
- Deep need to be close – to such a degree that they can overwhelm themselves and lead to a Five disappearing during a date
- Tendency to share their unique world with "the" chosen one or with those in very close relationships – associating the relationship with sharing secrets

If you relate to Type 5, these Instincts, in conjunction with your Object Relation, will lead to considerable demands on your partner to accom- pany you into your inner, frequently frightening, universe. You will seek truths about what it is to be human and have a tendency to scare your partner to see whether (s)he will follow you and stay by your side. The Rejection-relationship with both Figures will mean that you require or challenge your partner to demonstrate the qualities of both Figures, even as you observe whether your partner completely understands you.

Sexual – points to bear in mind

- Bear in mind that when you challenge those in close relationships with you to find out what they are thinking, feeling or "can man- age", you should share with them the fact that you are trying to understand them or get to know them
- Bear in mind that you can have a deep need for closeness and that you invest considerable energy in participating in bringing it about. Share this information with whomever you are with, so that you are *participating with them* – rather than *doing something to them*
- Bear in mind that you can end up entering into untenable rela- tionships (in both working and private contexts), which are not necessarily useful or healthy for you

Object Relation for Type 6

Type 6s have an Attachment-relationship with the Protective Figure, which means that they have an ambivalent or diffuse experience of the qualities expressed by the Protective Figure. They will therefore have a sense that there was no lack of "direction" in their childhood, but they also find it difficult to describe or explain how this was expressed.

Type 6 has a sense that it is possible to establish a clear and trans- parent direction (decision-making, clarification, or taking a stance) with regard to the important things in the world and therefore invests time in finding these clear, transparent answers, as well as in constructing prin- ciples or methods that support this sense of security. We see adult Sixes as full of doubt, and they have difficulty making clear and transparent choices – unless these are to do with topics about which they have pre- viously made choices and have thus already constructed explicit princi- ples around.

The young Six seeks clarity and transparent procedures in the world, and Sixes take this tendency with them into adulthood, compensating with a kind of emotional action when they encounter secure, rational and clear decision-making. Many Sixes are spontaneous, because spon- taneity dissolves their rational confusion – and they are thereby absolved from taking final decisions.

Close relationships

In close relationships – regardless of the other's Type – Sixes have a ten- dency to challenge their partner, to get the partner to make some of the decisions they find difficult themselves. This can happen directly, either by making a decision and waiting to see what their partner says to find out whether the partner agrees, or by not making a decision and await- ing the partner's reaction.

Points to bear in mind in close relationships

- When do you believe that mind-reading is possible, and what is your reaction when your partner does not perceive things in the same way as you?
- How will you know that you are secure in your close relationships?
- What do you gain by challenging those close to you – particularly with regard to big decisions?
- What does spontaneity do to you in your close relationships?

The Object Relation in all of us

The Attachment-relationship with the Protective Figure exists in all of us and is expressed by the fact that we yearn to feel secure in our decisions, and we do not want to be cheated because we have not thought our decisions through.

Instincts

Our Instincts also have a significant influence on the dynamics of our close relationships. There follows a brief description of the three Instincts characterising Type 6, along with a short guide to a range of points to bear in mind for the Type.

Self-preservation – tendencies

- Focus on resources – particularly in the domestic sphere
- Tendency to focus on work and building a secure world or daily routine through working procedures and the benefits deriving from work, such as money and seniority
- Often take responsibility for practical matters domestically, for instance paying bills, maintaining the car, making dental appointments for the children, and dealing with insurance
- Worry about trivialities, which can snowball into catastrophes
- Persevere with relationships – both private and in work contexts – that are dysfunctional; similarly, it takes a long time to form friendships (are you reliable?)

If you relate to Type 6, these Instincts, in conjunction with your Object Relation, will foster a significant need for certainty, peace of mind and security. You will probably be the one who takes over many of the practicalities in the relationship – and enjoy doing so. Your Object Relation also means that you believe in the existence of mind-reading, which is why you can be disappointed that your partner does not help in the right way at the right time. The Attachment-relationship with the Protective Figure leads you to want to put yourself forward as the Protective Figure, but at the same time you require your partner to fill in for you when you are worn out. The challenge here lies in the fact that your partner does not know when the time to fill in for you starts and ends.

Self-preservation – points to bear in mind
- Bear in mind that you can take too much responsibility upon yourself (both at work and at home) and can thus feel disappoint- ed when those around you do not appreciate or understand your efforts
- Bear in mind that you can overdramatise the consequences of small things, such as those arising from only having notes and not also coins for a trip to the flea market, the thought that there may not be a petrol station for the next 400 kilometres, or that some water on the kitchen table can cause the whole house to rot
- Bear in mind that you often spend your time thinking about your colleagues or family at the expense of your own needs

Social – tendencies
- Groups mean security; therefore Sixes seek out groups that represent security and stability
- Sixes construct relationships through warmth and friendliness (rather like Twos), and can use self-deprecation to build confidence and trust
- Tendency to insist that agreements be adhered to and obligations complied with (rather like Ones)
- Seek consensus rather than pursuing their own goals/dreams

- Can ally themselves with others, who might, for example, have been exploited by an ex-employer and may pursue a legal case alongside the person who has been exploited
- Pressure causes pessimism – a risk of fanaticism

If you relate to Type 6, these Instincts, in conjunction with your Object Relation, divert your attention away from your close relationship and lead you to focus on a single principle, movement or organisation, which then attracts a great deal of your attention. You may well be capable of transforming your shared home into a meeting place for the organisation that you chair and, given your belief in mind-reading, you are surprised when your partner is not quite in agreement with you that the choral society should practise at your place on Mondays, Wednesdays and Fri- days. You will have a tendency toward fanaticism, such that your Object Relation compels you to demand that your partner gives you space – and perhaps even requires your partner to speak positively about your com- mitment to a movement or organisation.

Social – points to bear in mind
- Bear in mind that it can be to your advantage to listen more to either your feelings or your intuition – or a combination of both, which might be termed your emotional intuition or your intuitive feelings
- Bear in mind that you can take a more mellow, playful or experi- mental approach to the way in which you fulfil your tasks
- Bear in mind that you have great "warmth", and this can be used to see things in a rather better light. Your warm spirits are infectious!

Sexual – tendencies
- Seek a robust, steadfast and strong mate who can create the secu- rity they look for
- Find intimacy by focussing on physical strength and robustness – and conceal insecurity through assertiveness or by challenging authority (rather like Eights)

- Find security in those they are close to, who must, however, by no means let the Six down or hold different convictions
- Tend to turn against those close to them if they feel threatened
- Sceptical about others and can experience powerful emotional reactions if they feel under attack

If you relate to Type 6, these Instincts, in conjunction with your Object Relation, generate a very strong focus on that type of close relationship whereby you generally have only one close relationship, such as only your spouse, only your child, only your colleague, or only your boss. Your Object Relation will mean that you more or less take over the qualities of the Protective Figure in the relationship – and you can thus seem rather like an Eight in terms of your energy, dedication and appearance. It will be easy for you to challenge your partner in order to ensure that they have considered matters thoroughly and are indeed still committed to the relationship.

Sexual – points to bear in mind
- Bear in mind that your energy can make you seem too robust, persistent, self-secure or overbearing
- Bear in mind that you have a tendency to seem dominating or controlling with others. This can be mistaken for jealousy, but it is more about you wanting to feel secure in your relationship
- Bear in mind that you have a craving for freedom that pushes others away – at the same time as you want your relationship to be close.

The Object Relation for Type 7

Type 7 has a Frustration-relationship with the Nurturing Figure, mean- ing that the Figure was present and was actually in a position to provide the qualities represented by the Nurturing Figure, but that they were not provided or presented completely, clearly and consistently. It was, then, possible for the Seven to experience, for example, care and peace of mind via the Nurturing Figure, just not in the way the young Seven would have liked; this created the frustration that accompanies the Sev- en throughout the rest of his/her life.

Type 7s are fully aware that it is in fact possible to be in close con- tact with themselves, those close to them and with life itself, and they attempt to find or to bring out that ease in life that arises when one is unconditionally loved. This often happens by encountering life through experiences or activities that are dressed up as play – the closest we can get to a worry-free existence, completely surrounded by love and trust. Naturally, it is difficult to recreate the naïve, playful and happy condi- tions of childhood, yet it is precisely this re-creation, or an imitation of it, that Sevens attempt to perform through their many activities.

In the experience of the young Seven, then, the qualities from the Nur- turing Figure are inconsistent and not to be trusted; this is the founda- tion for the Seven's deep desire for it to be possible one day to bask in a profound existential conversation, preferably with their partner. The fulfilment of this desire is often hindered by the Seven him/herself be- cause of a lack of patience and a lack of experience in engaging in deep- er conversation. Therefore, the fantasies that become characteristic of the Seven's personality, about how contentment or happiness can be achieved, come into being, and can result in a quest for satisfying experi- ences which quickly lose their appeal when the Seven tries them, before moving rapidly on to the next prospective activity.

Close relationships

In close relationships – regardless of the other's Type – Sevens have a natural frustration about their partner not being cheerful, lively and fun, and for not getting involved in energising activities. In terms of their partner, the thought that there could be something more exciting out there becomes an albatross around the Seven's neck, since the quest for the new and exciting can take over. Their restlessness can also take the form of condescending and withering comments about their partner's or child's abilities.

Points to bear in mind in close relationships

- How are you completely attentive and fully present with your partner?
- What expectations do you have of your partner about being energetic, lively, active and supportive of your ideas and projects?
- What do you want your partner to see in you, bring out of you or discover about you?
- How are you the one that disturbs or distracts yourself and your partner in creating a deep and close relationship?

The Object Relation in all of us

The Frustration-relationship with the Nurturing Figure exists in all of us, and it is expressed by means of our distracting ourselves and those close to us when conversations become too intense, serious, painful or deep. However, we all long for meaningful discussions, but we often have a tendency to lose attention if these do not move on quickly enough or if they begin to lose their vigour.

Instincts

Our Instincts also have a significant influence on the dynamics of our close relationships. There follows a brief description of the three Instincts characterising Type 7, along with a short guide to a range of points to bear in mind for the Type.

Self-preservation – tendencies

- Expend their energy and decisiveness on securing their own needs and well-being – often have high levels of consumption
- Can make lists of all the lovely things they would like to own or do
- Tend to use working life to create the security they need to live a life full of possibility
- Want freedom and independence, particularly in close relationsh ips
- Tendency toward a physical need for things (food, warmth, repay- ment of borrowed money), and can experience mounting frustra- tion if their needs are not fulfilled – if this need-fulfilment is the obligation of someone else
- May be ruthless in maintaining security

If you relate to Type 7, these Instincts, in conjunction with your Object Relation, give you a propensity to consume more, and you will have a tendency to focus on your financial resources. If you and your partner have shared finances, you will in all likelihood experience considera- ble frustration over the things your partner spends money on, even as you shower resources on buying things that seemed magical – when you were in the shop. You will fight for your freedoms, including your economic freedom, and, with this Object Relation, you will be deeply frustrated (borderline powerless and furious) if your partner does not understand your need for personal freedom.

Self-preservation – points to bear in mind

- Bear in mind that your aspirations and lust for "experiences" can limit, restrict or actually damage those you care about
- Bear in mind that you can push those close to you away if you feel that they are restricting you – particularly if they are only trying to be close to you
- Bear in mind that you may have a tendency to ignore your own feelings, both positive and negative. So if you would like to fully

enjoy your experiences, you will need the capacity to immerse yourself in all forms of feeling

Social – tendencies

- Have many arrangements for the same Saturday evening
- Tend to spread their energy around start-up projects, brainstorm- ing sessions, exciting/occult/séance gatherings or activities – which rarely come to fruition
- Tend to gather groups together that share the same needs or inter- ests
- Enjoy being stimulated in social contexts – and have a tendency to "move on" when the group no longer supplies the right energy or stimulation, or when things come to a standstill
- Do not care for authority, which can seem restrictive and unnec- essary

If you relate to Type 7, these Instincts, in conjunction with your Object Relation, will shift your focus away from your close relationship toward the many ways relationships can be formed with, for example, friends, clients, colleagues and festival-goers. You will seek out energy from ex- ternal relationships and perhaps feel that your close relationship is rath- er tame and lacks energy – and you may have a tendency to feel that you are trapped in this relationship. You will look for energy in your groups or create positive energy in external relationships, while demanding that your partner gives you the space to enjoy and live your life.

Social – points to bear in mind

- Bear in mind that you can have a tendency to manipulate those around you with your ardour, energy and enthusiasm
- Note when you are too harsh on yourself in your desire to be something for other people (or to be someone who encourages others). Realise that this is a completely acceptable desire that should not be ridiculed
- Bear in mind that you can be someone who is a "good-time junk-

ie", who only wants to be with others when they are in top form and are doing well – and who moves on if they are having a bad time or need you to engage with them

Sexual – tendencies

- Seek intensity in other people and can let their imagination run riot regarding all the excitement they will have with the very spe- cial people in their lives
- Love wild ideas and may idealise themselves and their relation-ships
- Try to be with interesting people – and tend not to have interests of their own
- Love to fall in love and to lose themselves in love – but afraid of commitment
- Think quickly, which can make them restless in relation to them-selves
- Seek extreme stimuli

If you relate to Type 7, these Instincts, in conjunction with your Object Relation, will generate in you a powerful urge for your partner to notice you, to accommodate you and to bring out your qualities.

You will require your partner to be attentive and sufficiently focussed to enable you to discover yourself, even though the reality is that it is often you who distract yourself away from attentiveness. Your partner should provide magical and exciting energy, and you will have a tenden- cy to plan a magical weekend with your partner, whereby the planning (imaginary) is more interesting than actually being with your partner for a WHOLE WEEKEND! Frustration with the Nurturing Figure will find its expression in your demand that your partner supplies precisely that (loving) energy, which makes literally just you happy.

Sexual – points to bear in mind

- Bear in mind that your fine mind may well invent "solid" rational arguments in favour of overconsumption or get lost in ideas about how things should be (work, relationships etc.)

- Bear in mind that you may have a tendency to fantasise about events and get stuck in your fantasy rather than reality
- Bear in mind that your frustration (the idea that you could get what you want but are prevented from getting it) may take control of your behaviour

The Object Relation for Type 8

Type 8 has a Rejection-relationship with the Nurturing Figure, which means that the Figure was non-existent, the result of which was that the Eight did not mirror and get to practise the qualities inherent in the Nurturing Figure. Therefore, a great many Eights have difficulty expressing unconditional love and trust – and, as a rule, need to make demands or set conditions for how love or trust ought to be built up.

Type 8 thus had difficulties mastering the qualities from the Nurturing Figure, but instead focussed fully on the qualities of the Protective Fig- ure. This means that the adult Eight masters the art of saying "yes" and "no", making demands and establishing limits. The Eight has a tendency to take over responsibility and to be the one driving or carrying the rela- tionship – both domestically and in the workplace. On the other hand, this also means that they stumble when it comes to showing empathy or giving themselves unconditionally – in relation to themselves, adults in close relationships and their children.

The young Eight builds up a robustness and steeliness that shields a vulnerable, innocent and naïve heart; many Eights say that their body is always tense and prepared to fight. They therefore construct a personali- ty around a physically strong body, able to withstand and deal with exer- tion, while they also develop a (strategic) sense for who is where within the hierarchy, who knows who, and how to go about gaining or regaining power. Emotional qualities are developed later than bodily and relation- al qualities.

Close relationships

In close relationships – regardless of the other's Type – the Eight makes considerable demands of their partner, such that their love resembles unconditional love. That is, the partner must cherish the Eight unconditionally, no matter how the Eight behaves. The unconditional love that resides within the Nurturing Figure – and which the Eight typically did not experience during childhood – tends be supplied by the partner dur- ing adulthood.

Points to bear in mind in close relationships

- What demands do you make in your close relationships, and what are the consequences if they are not met?
- How do you pressurise or punish your partner, and how do you figure that you benefit from this pressure or punishment?
- How do you gain from having the last word in a discussion with your partner?
- How is it useful for you to take responsibility away from your partner?
- What is difficult for you about showing unconditional love to, care for and confidence in your partner?

The Object Relation in all of us

The Rejection-relationship with the Nurturing Figure resides in all of us and finds its expression in our having difficulty showing uncondition- al love to, care for and confidence in other people, including those we feel close to. Placing our destiny in the hands of others by opening up to them, by revealing who we are, and by allowing them to know us com- pletely is difficult for most people.

Instincts

Our Instincts also have a significant influence on the dynamics of our close relationships. There follows a brief description of the three Instincts characterising Type 8, along with a short guide to a range of points to bear in mind for the Type.

Self-preservation – tendencies

- Intense focus on money to ensure that there is sufficient money

and power
- Create rules for what is "yours" and "mine" – including in the private sphere
- Find security through their place within the hierarchy and seek financial security as evidence for this placement
- Focus on security; it should be they who build this security for themselves and for those around them
- Take the view that it is OK to cover their needs – and go after what is "theirs"

If you relate to Type 8, these Instincts, in conjunction with your Object Relation, will sharpen your focus upon what is yours, and if you live in the western world, this will be about money and the things that are at your disposal. Money will give you peace of mind and security, and you will try to downplay your need for money by saying to yourself that the most sensible course of action is to have one's own money in case a situ- ation should arise in which it is necessary to look after yourself. You will find it difficult to tolerate your partner not sharing this viewpoint, and your Object Relation will result in a very low level of empathy for and identification with your partner.

Self-preservation – points to bear in mind
- Bear in mind that you can be too rigid about what is yours – par- ticularly in the private sphere. Explain to those close to you what this is about and your intentions in having "yours"
- Bear in mind that you have a tendency to focus too much on the question of who decides, whether you have power and freedom, and whether you are in the right location within the hierarchy. You might find yourself appearing much more dominant than you intend
- Bear in mind that you seem like someone to whom others do not want to tell the truth

Social – tendencies

- Demand tight bonds in their close relationships – happily reveal secrets about themselves, and require that those close to them should also reveal theirs
- Tendency to decide who should be "in" and who should be "out" of the network – may test their relationships
- Very energetic in social contexts and like to "bring in" those people they believe would belong in their groups
- Tend to feel a sense of prestige by being with the right people – this creates a form of security with regard to placement within the hierarchy
- Exaggerate their past and their achievements
- Often predictable relationships – can bear a grudge
- Strong feelings and heated discussions – can you take the heat?

If you relate to Type 8, these Instincts, in conjunction with your Object Relation, will give you all the care, attention and love you could possibly need outside your close relationships. You will have a fixed idea about where you are located within the hierarchy, both privately and professionally. If you regard yourself as the one who is responsible for earning money for your family, you will take this role extremely seriously and go the extra mile to fulfil it. You will require your partner to acknowledge the enormous effort that you make, while your partner must also allow you to carry out your work in precisely the way you regard as being correct.

Social – points to bear in mind

- Bear in mind that you have a tendency to exaggerate your achievements – with the frequent result that you appear false or superficial
- Bear in mind that you have a tendency to prove that you are "a real man" or "a woman that can take the heat". It can appear overblown or a sign of "weakness" that you need to proclaim your manhood in a masculine or feminine version

- Bear in mind that you see yourself as the assembly point for those close to you and have the notion that people would not meet un- less you invite them to the party or gathering.

Sexual – tendencies

- Tendency to crave intimacy and passion – which may end up becoming too demanding for the partner
- Can be deeply engaging and loving, but may also regard intimacy as a battle for control
- Enjoy being the "bad guy", as this creates intensity and brings out the rebel in the Eight
- Enjoy wild passion in relationships, which can easily burn out
- Tendency to feel a sense of ownership in close relationships, and have a fierce temperament and jealousy – may be harsh and impatient

If you relate to Type 8, this Instinct, in conjunction with your Object Re- lation, will give you an extremely intense (perhaps even intimidating) energy, and you will demand that your partner shares your passionate and intimate energy, and that your partner also provides the same to you. You will feel good about doing things together physically, while playing tennis, running or gardening together will give you a sense that you belong together and are in the fight together. The rebel in you of- ten emerges when you either provoke your partner or provoke or rebuke other diners in the restaurant if they are unpleasant toward the staff. And you will of course require your partner to permit your behaviour, even though you may well enjoy the fact that your partner is also provoked or scared by you rebuking the other diners.

Sexual – points to bear in mind

- Bear in mind that you can be extremely intense in your close relationships and demand that your partner can also provide the same intensity. A sense of shared intensity will often be a quality you need in love

- Bear in mind that you can go too far in your (working and private) relationships in order to get them to function
- Bear in mind that you are prone to using this energy or intimacy as a resource to get what you want. This means that those around you can mistake your attentiveness for aggression

The Object Relation for Type 9

Type 9 has an Attachment-relationship with both Figures, which means that the qualities residing in both Figures were a part of the Nine's child- hood, although diffusely and in a way that the Nine was ambivalent about. The Nine felt loved and cared about, and had a clear and defi- nite framework for life in a way that is unclear and which they cannot explain or describe. In practice, this means that most things in life (in- cluding everything residing within the Protective and Nurturing Figures) are diffuse or unclear, and it can be difficult for the Nine to take a view on whether they have a good relationship, or whether it is moving in the right direction.

Fundamentally, Type 9s feel that relationships are positive and good, as well as feeling that they will, in all likelihood, arrive at a place in life where things are good. Many Nines also have a sense that they will live to be over 100: they will enjoy a long life, so they will have enough time to come into contact with everything that is meaningful. This often results in them delaying crucial decisions or waiting to withdraw from essential relationships (in private and working contexts).

The young Nine has, in many ways, a carefree existence and does not necessarily take a position with regard to the big questions or about life's great issues. As adults, they will have "gone with the flow" and landed wherever it is pleasant and not too demanding for them. They will have lived life intuitively, even though it has not been easy to listen to their gut feelings. They therefore generally live life through emotional catalysts, and the exercise of their emotional faculties has led them to discover educa- tional courses, relationships or jobs that seemed interesting to them.

Close relationships

In close relationships – regardless of the other's Type – the Nine takes a relaxed approach to his/her partner and is tolerant about the relation- ship, as long as the partner does not make demands. This positive, intu- itive, light and forward-looking flow within the partnership supplies the tranquillity to make discoveries along the way and to gradually take a position with regard to things as they evolve.

Points to bear in mind in close relationships

- When do you think that mind-reading is possible, and what is your reaction to your partner not perceiving things in the way that you do?
- How do you romanticise your relationship with your partner, and how do you react when reality does not match your dream/fanta- sy?
- What happens when you withdraw into your inner universe?
- What are the challenges involved in expressing yourself clearly and in sharing precisely and directly how you feel and what you need?
- What do you achieve by being passive or indecisive in your close relationships?

The Object Relation in all of us

The Attraction-relationship with both Figures resides in all of us and finds its expression in the difficulty we can have in being sure of our pre- cise direction in life, and in that we can find it more pleasant not to take a position on this issue. We can also find it difficult to have a close relation- ship with ourselves, and it can be easier not to take a position on who we are and why we are what we are.

Instincts

Our Instincts also have a significant influence on the dynamics of our close relationships. There follows a brief description of the three Instincts characterising Type 9, along with a short guide to a range of points to bear in mind for the Type.

Self-preservation – tendencies

- Easily become grudging, passive-aggressive or tacitly resistant
- Tendency to seek lesser, easier tasks – rather than more demanding, ambitious projects
- Enjoy simple solutions with well-rehearsed activities and routines – treading a well-worn path
- Seek physical comfort and serenity – small rewards
- Lack ambition, but talented – stifle their own real needs
- Block out unpleasant feelings or experiences

If you relate to Type 9, these Instincts, in conjunction with your Object Relation, make you more comfortable, passive and patient. The Instincts create a need to look after your resources, while the Object Relation creates a need not to feel encroached upon. Together, these provide an en- ergy that may well generate a lot of movement…without really getting anywhere. You will therefore require your partner not to disturb you too much, as this would be regarded as an encroachment and would result only in even more inactivity and silence from you.

Self-preservation – points to bear in mind

- Bear in mind that you often make your protests through passivity or indecision. This is an effective means of getting your way, but you can destroy relationships that way
- Bear in mind that you have a tendency to relax in your own company by doing nothing. This can become such a comfortable and natural state that it can be difficult to spring into action when it really matters
- Bear in mind that you hold back on many conversations that could be useful to get started

Social – tendencies

- Have difficulty saying "no" to people from the group and may disappear within the group
- Tendency to be active around the group but also to be emotional-

ly closed-down
- Enjoy being with others in the easiest way without obligations
- Use the group as a place to hide away
- Passive-aggressive methods to oppose others – absent-minded and disillusioned

If you relate to Type 9, these Instincts, in conjunction with your Object Relation, will mean that you are likely to disappear within the groups of which you are a part. In practice, this will result in you preferring to be at work with your colleagues than with those you have close relationships with. You will be able to hide within groups and, if you are fortunate, you will be able to position yourself in such a way that the other group members (colleagues, for example) demand nothing of you. Your Object Relation also leads you to believe in the existence of mind-reading, so that you wonder why your partner cannot figure out that you get more energy from going to work, going to football practice with friends or being on a trip with the hiking society.

Social – points to bear in mind
- Bear in mind that you have a tendency to hide in the group, which can mean that others begin to take you for granted or exclude you from decision-making
- Bear in mind that you stifle your own views and values – particularly in workplace relationships, so that you overuse your private sphere to bring out your frustrations
- Bear in mind that you can create disharmony or imbalance precisely because you do not share your views with others

Sexual – tendencies
- Tendency to pair up with "the one and only", and, once this has been done…well then, everything is settled for ever
- Idealise close relationships and avoid mentioning flaws or deficiencies within them
- Build a life together with their partner, whereupon they them-

selves disappear in the desire for an "us"

- May start focussing on earlier relationships, which seem to have been more comfortable
- When they compliment or censure others, it is in fact themselves they are talking about!

If you relate to Type 9, these Instincts, in conjunction with your Object Relation, will create a powerful sense of being with the "one and only". You will go the extra mile to get the relationship to work, and if there are children in the relationship, it will verge on the impossible to dissolve the relationship, no matter how unhealthy it may be for you. This ide- alisation of the relationship may also extend to previous relationships, about which you construct an internal fantasy about how wonderful it is to be in a relationship. You will also require your partner to disappear into your relationship – thereby effectively dissolving each other in fa- vour of a common identity.

Sexual – points to bear in mind

- Bear in mind that you very quickly become content with a rela- tionship (working or private) and that relationships need to be constantly developed to be sustainable
- Bear in mind that you may find yourself adopting a different outlook on life and a different set of values, and thereby lose the sense of what you should do with your life
- Bear in mind that you can get caught up in memories of how it was to have a different boss, different colleagues or a different lover

RELATIONSHIPS BETWEEN THE ENNEAGRAM TYPES

In the same way as we all mirrored ourselves in our close relationships as we grew up, we continue this form of reflection in our adult relationships. We mirrored ourselves in our essential close relationships when we were younger, and we thereby developed skills, habits and convictions based upon these reflections. This also means that we have particular ideas about the Figures in which we mirrored ourselves and, accordingly, cer- tain expectations. As adults, we project ourselves in our essential close relationships, consisting typically of our romantic partners. A large part of our personality often errs in thinking that these partners should meet the expectations we had of our Nurturing and/or Protective Figure in our childhood. These expectations often cause misunderstandings, frustra- tions and sometimes breakdowns in our relationships – as well as perhaps forming part of the "incorrect" reasoning behind entering into a relation- ship, based on the belief that we can have certain expectations met.

If we combine all the Enneagram Types with each other, we get 45 dif- ferent Type-combinations, all of which behave in a specific way in close relationships. As each Type is partly moulded on the structure within the Object Relations, there will be many explanations to uncover in the dynamics between the Types by drawing upon their expectations of each other that arise through their Object Relations. The following descrip- tions of the 45 Type-couples therefore include accounts of when the Types inspire each other, when they irritate each other, and what each partner can particularly focus on or work with in order to develop them- selves in the relationship. It is worth noting here that this book does not attempt to explain *how* one should work on the areas it is fruitful to work on; the purpose of the book is to point out a definite direction to take in order to promote personal development..

Relationship between Type 1 and Type 1

Description of the relationship when both partners feel resourceful

When their interaction is enriching, supportive, inspiring and evolving, the two Ones will be respectful and tolerant toward each other. They will both contribute to a relationship in which they support each other to create structures and cultivate/sustain their principles, and they will find a way to maintain their individual integrity, while also standing to- gether and backing each other up.

They will both contribute to a relationship in which their higher values, rules and principles are maintained, even though they will occasionally disagree. Both will have a mission that is higher than themselves, and in their relationship they will help each other to live out their respective missions.

From the outside, the relationship is regarded as principled, disci- plined, dedicated, and characterised by high ethical and moral stand- ards, as well as integrity.

Description of the relationship when both partners feel under pressure

When their interaction is restrictive, accusatory, destructive and demo- tivating, both Ones will be frustrated that the other does not follow the correct principles and that the other makes such obviously wrong deci- sions. They will constantly encounter their own dark side because the other is too narrow-minded, uncompromising in his/her principles, in- flexible, blind, intransigent and self-righteous. They will instil in the oth- er a feeling of being wrong, slovenly or irresponsible, which are precisely those things the One fears in him/herself.

Description of the measures that may bring the partners closer to each other

Both Ones have their own high principles concerning how to be in a relationship with each other, and both work hard to ensure that their part- ner understands and conforms to these principles. This is inevitably an insoluble task, and when they begin to be critical and censorious toward each other, the response is also critical and censorious. They both have a Frustration-relationship with the Protective Figure and attempt to im- port principles and rules into the relationship in order to get the rela- tionship to function. At the same time, their principles and rules are part of the One's identity, so, if they are to relax their rules and principles, it is necessary for them to work at the level of their identity, which is an extremely difficult task. However, when the One-couple do manage to evolve together, they will have worked through critical elements of their (often traumatic) habits and patterns in connection with their Object Re- lation. That is to say, in practice, that the One will discover that the world is not wrong and that it is not their job to fix things so that these things are right or correct.

It is recommended that they work on developing flexibility and cu- riosity, while investigating where precisely the Object Relation can be that place where they achieve the great breakthrough in their personal development.

Relationship between Type 1 and Type 2

Description of the relationship when both partners feel resourceful

When their interaction is enriching, supportive, inspiring and evolving, the One will be tender and sincere, while the Two will be empathic and supportive. Typically, the Two will bring out the more relationship-oriented side of the One, while the One will inspire discipline and durabil- ity. The Two will also contribute to the relationship with warm-hearted- ness, self-acceptance and self-worth, while the One will contribute with stability, boundaries and trust. Both Types will mutually contribute to caring responsibilities, and both will have a particular focus on others. Outside the relationship, this focus may be on work, charity or interper- sonal help and assistance. This external focus also applies to themselves as individuals, such that interaction has less meaning for themselves as a couple or individually.

From outside, the relationship is likely to be perceived as serious, sta- ble, responsible, caring and hard-working.

Description of the relationship when both partners feel under pressure

When their interaction is restrictive, accusatory, destructive and demoti- vating, the One will feel overwhelmed by the Two's need for recognition and physical contact. Conversely, the Two will take the One's sarcasm and "sharp tongue" as a personal attack. Typically, One will show loyalty to a cause, while Two's loyalty is located within the relationship.

Type 1 will often feel that they have worked hard, sparing no effort, and have therefore earned the right to certain privileges. There can therefore be a tendency to take the Two for granted and expect the Two to support the One in the application of the latter's principles. Type 2 has difficul- ties with expressing their own needs and first feels properly loved when, unprompted, the One expresses the appreciation to which the Two feels entitled.

Description of the measures that may bring the partners closer to each other

Both partners have a marked tendency to expect that the other can figure out by him/herself what needs to be done to satisfy them. Type 1's sense of entitlement prevents the One from clearly expressing their expecta- tions or wants, while Type 2's pride holds them back from expressing their needs or wants. Both Types have issues with their inner Protective Figure: early in his/her childhood, the One felt compelled to forge their own strong inner Protective Figure; in the Two's experience, there was no Protective Figure to mirror him/herself in and the Two has not there- fore properly learned the skill of withdrawing, establishing boundaries or expressing his/her own needs.

It is recommended that the One works on their self-entitlement and that the Two works on giving expression to their own needs.

Relationship between Type 1 and Type 3

Description of the relationship when both partners feel resourceful

When the interaction is enriching, supportive, inspiring and evolving, the One will be diligent and inspiring, while the Three will be team-ori- ented and realistic. Typically, the Three will inspire the One to be pleased with those situations in which 80 percent is good enough, while the One will provide the inspiration to work through the final details to ensure that everything is fully completed. At the same time, the Three will con- tribution to a relationship with ambition, originality and the implemen- tation of values, while the One's contribution will be order, quality and warmth, helping the Three to accept the "home truths" that the One can often provide by way of feedback to the Three.

Both Types will work hard to work out their values together, and they will focus sharply on achieving their objectives in their activities and on making a difference. Their relationship will often concentrate on their professional work, and together they will inspire each other to work for a good cause or projects that have great meaning for others. They also have the ability to maintain high levels of energy and momentum, praise each other for their accomplishments, and both are happy to receive feedback with a view to being even better, sharper or more insightful in their pro- fessional field.

Viewed from outside, the relationship is likely to be perceived as goal-oriented, excellent, idealistic, secure, professional and proud.

Description of the relationship when both partners feel under pressure

When the interaction is restrictive, accusatory, destructive and demotivating, the One will experience the Three as irresponsible, as someone who embellishes the truth, and who all too quickly alters their goals or opinions. Conversely, the Three will find the One far too mentally and creatively limited, rigidly adhering to fixed principles, and stubborn. Typically, the One will follow his/her principles, while the Three will fol- low a path to a solution.

At the start, the Type 1 will suppress their frustration with the Three, and when it is finally aired, it will be through sarcasm and uncompro- mising condemnation. This will be taken as a personal attack by the Three, who will therefore begin to mistrust the One. The Three will con- sider themselves better than the One and downplay the importance of the One's comments, frustrating the One to the extent that frustration becomes anger. Both have a blind faith in their own abilities, which often results in a mistrust of the abilities of the other.

Description of the measures that may bring the partners closer to each other

Both partners approach a pressurised situation rationally, although both shut the other out emotionally. Type 1 has a Frustration-relationship with the Protective Figure and attempts to stick to his/her principles and rules, while Type 3 experiences ambivalence in his/her relation to the Nurturing Figure, making it difficult for the Three to respect the relation- ship. In practice, this means that the One will "die" for his/her princi- ples, while the Three becomes indifferent toward the relationship. As the Three starts to "go solo", the One will continue fighting for exactly those principles that may, for the One, pertain to relationships, solidarity and loyalty. It can seem that the One is burning with frustration, spite and anger, while the Three is moving on to new assignments and activities, leaving the One to his/her "death spiral".

It is recommended that Type 1 works on loosening their grip on their principles, and that Type 3 works on remaining within the relationship and enduring the One's frustrations and accusations.

Relationship between Type 1 and Type 4

Description of the relationship when both partners feel resourceful

When the interaction is enriching, supportive, inspiring and evolving, the One will be complimentary and supportive, while the Four will be playful and gentle. Typically, the One will bring out the more stable and trusting side of the Four, while the Four will inspire a combination of airiness/lightness and profundity, and will help in the One's search for the essential/real.

Both Types will contribute to the quest for the essential as well as living up to the real and meaningful. This focus on the essential can foster a natural solidarity, and both partners can experience the things that are essential to them. This can bring about a natural solidarity, although with the possibility of disagreements about where the focus should be with regard to specifics and when a shared focus on the relationship should come into view.

Viewed from outside, the relationship is perceived as close-knit, vibrant, genuine, experimental and dedicated.

Description of the relationship when both partners feel under pressure

When the interaction is restrictive, accusatory, destructive and demotivating, the One will feel provoked by the Four's need for attention and by their irresponsibility and unreasonable grandstanding. Conversely, the Four feels restricted by One's principles and rules about the correct way to behave and the correct path to follow. Type 1s have a tendency to pur- sue a cause that is bigger than themselves, while Fours take on causes that are like their own, or which take their starting point in themselves.

Type 1 will often have the feeling that it is they that go the extra mile in the relationship and therefore indirectly have the right to criticise or admonish the Four. But precisely this admonition is not necessarily exactly what is required to stimulate the Four in a close relationship. Type 4 will have a tendency to confront the One, telling them all the ways in which they also do not match the wishes that the Four has with regard to their partner; the One will take this as a pointed personal criticism.

Description of the measures that may bring the partners closer to each other

The inner critic that is characteristic of the One will convince them that they are correct in their understandings and assertions, so they have a tendency to direct their internal frustration toward the Four. The Four's inner critic is far more destructive and inclined to depression than the One's inner critic, and the fallout that results lasts much longer than is the case for the One. Type One has a Frustration-relationship with the Protective Figure, while the Four has a Frustration-relationship with both Figures. As a result, this frustration and powerlessness, alongside the effort put into getting the other to change, can contribute to making the relationship fragile.

It is recommended that Type 1 should work on how to give criticism/feedback, given their relationship with the Four, and that the Four work on figuring out when they make unreasonable and often unfair demands of the One.

Relationship between Type 1 and Type 5

Description of the relationship when both partners feel resourceful

When the interaction is enriching, supportive, inspiring and evolving, the One will feel playful and vibrant, while the Five will be precise and able to relate. Typically, the One will bring out the easy-going Five, while the Five will inspire sober new thinking, where "sober" is understood to mean substantiated and responsible. The One will contribute both gravity and playfulness to the relationship, while the Five will contribute with new ways of looking at the obvious. Both Types will contribute to an inquisitive, playful, experimental and precise energy, whereby together they will acquire a renewed enthusiasm for investing in a deeper insight into or development of a topic. There is not as much attention paid to the relationship itself as to the real, the valid, the valued or the meaningful.

Viewed from outside, the relationship is perceived as childlike/naive, persistent, lost (that is, lost in work, a hobby or a cause), abstract and yet goal-oriented and specific.

Description of the relationship when both partners feel under pressure

When the relationship is restrictive, accusatory, destructive and demo-tivating, the One will feel frustrated at how quickly the Five shuts down the relationship or dialogue, or loses interest. Conversely, the Five be- comes tired of the One's assumed and "in no way substantiated" truths. Typically, the One devotes him/herself to principles and opinions, while the Five is convinced that both principles and opinions are mental con- structions that can be questioned and, when seen in a different light, can have completely opposite meanings.

Type 1 has principles regarding how the relationship should function and often misconstrues the Five's silence as a tacit acceptance of the One's principles. The Five also has principles and opinions, but these are more flexible and questioning than those of the One, and the Five has a tendency to let the One "stew in their own juices" – that is, in their all- too-quick decisions and opinions.

Description of the measures that may bring the partners closer to each other

This relationship has a tendency to devote itself to something, such as a principle, a cause, a professional field, but the couple do so in very differ- ent ways. While Ones are simple and straightforward in their principles, Fives will substantiate and argue for theirs. Discussions and arguments are not necessarily the One's strong point, as they often end up taking a situation personally, but Fives are fantastic at keeping their cool in a de- bate. Type 1s have a Frustration-relationship with the Protective Figure, meaning that they become frustrated when the Five does not operate in the same black and white terms as they do. Type 5s have a Rejection-re- lationship with the Protective Figure and are therefore relatively ambiv- alent about whether they are right or not, but they are provoked by the One's (uninformed) stubbornness.

It is recommended that Type 1 works on their taking things personally in discussions and that Type 5 works on saying more about their view- point rather than having a discussion for the sake of a discussion.

Relationship between Type 1 and Type 6

Description of the relationship when both partners feel resourceful

When the interaction is enriching, supportive, inspiring and evolving, the One will be lucid and able to relate to the other, while the Six will be supportive and helpful. Typically, the One will bring out the more precise and courageous aspects of the Six, while the Six will inspire col- laboration and dialogue. At the same time, the One will contribute with simplicity, while the Six will bring interaction.

Both Types will contribute to a dedicated, collaborative, loyal and re- sponsible relationship and will focus on solidarity or the principles be- hind solidarity. Typically, the One will work for a higher principle, while the Six focusses on a cause or a movement (such as the scout movement).

Viewed from outside, the relationship is perceived as loyal, stable, principally focused on what is "right" or, for example, on voluntary work.

Description of the relationship when both partners feel under pressure

When the interaction is restrictive, accusatory, destructive and demoti- vating, the One will be frustrated with Six's indecisiveness and "yes and no" approach, while the Six will feel powerless in the face of the One's (all too) rapid decisions. There is a tendency toward mistrust in this relation- ship, whereby the One cannot get to grips with the Six's way of challeng- ing the One within the relationship, and the Six may be insecure about whether the One is really fully committed to the relationship.

The One will have a principled dedication to the relationship itself, while the Six is dedicated to the solidarity within the relationship. There will be a tendency for the One to feel that they work hard for the relationship itself and to accuse the Six of not doing likewise, while the Six takes on a lot of tasks at home, without telling the One about it – and, as such, does not make an issue of the One not helping.

Description of the measures that may bring the partners closer to each other

When Sixes are fighting for solidarity or for their relationship, they can blind themselves as to whether it is healthy even to be in the relation- ship. Ones will act on their intuition much more quickly, and will make demands and be consistent. This consistency is not the Six's strong point, unless it is 100 percent clear that there is nothing left to fight for. Threats may therefore emerge from the One, which the Six spends an inordinate amount of time trying to understand or relate to. Type 1 has a Frustra- tion-relationship with the Protective Figure, while the Six has an Attach- ment-relationship with this Figure. As such, conflict will often occur in this relationship, revolving around principles, causes, relationships, and how to live up to or foster these principles or causes together.

It is recommended that Type 1 works on their criticism of the Six's causes and works on their own causes to a greater extent, while the Six works on being in the relationship on the right premises.

Relationship between Type 1 and Type 7

Description of the relationship when both partners feel resourceful

When the interaction is enriching, supportive, inspiring and evolving, the One will be experimental and energetic, while the Seven will be grateful and appreciative. Typically, the One will bring out the more profound side of the Seven, while the Seven will inspire with more light-hearted- ness and playfulness. At the same time, the One will contribute sharp- ness and clarity to the relationship, while the Seven will contribute with initiative and curiosity. Both Types will contribute to an appreciative and inquisitive relationship, in which the focus is action, openness and the job or assignment in hand. There is not necessarily an inner focus on the relationship itself particularly, but more on the job or assignment.

Viewed from outside, the relationship is likely to be perceived as both serious and infantile, tender, loving and task- or job-focussed.

Description of the relationship when both partners feel under pressure

When the interaction is restrictive, accusatory, destructive and demoti- vating, the One will be deeply frustrated with the Seven's many (ridicu- lous) fancies and impulses. The Seven's lack of concentration will frus- trate the One, and when the Seven is condescending and sarcastic, the One will take it deeply personally and remember it for ever. The Seven has a corresponding tendency toward frustration, which relates to the One's rigidity, all-too-high self-regard and the deep sense of self-entitle- ment residing within the One.

Type One will absolutely dedicate themselves to the relationship, while the Seven seems more flexible and less dedicated. The truth is that the partners display their dedication in two very different ways: Ones have their principles and Sevens their gratitude.

Description of the measures that may bring the partners closer to each other

Both Types are Frustration Types, but the One's relationship pertains to the Protective Figure, while the Seven's pertains to the Nurturing Figure. As such, both partners want something from the other which is impos- sible for the other to supply, a situation that creates deep frustration in both partners. Recall that the frustration comes from being able to see something one would like to have without being able to get it. Here, the Seven can see that it is possible to receive the qualities that the Nurtur- ing Figure represents in the One, and the One can see that it is possible to receive the protective qualities in the Seven – even as neither of the partners actually get what they want.

It is recommended that Type 1 works on his/her elevated sense of self-entitlement and that Type 7 works on his/her disenchanted emp- tiness.

Relationship between Type 1 and Type 8

Description of the relationship when both partners feel resourceful

When the interaction is enriching, supportive, inspiring and evolving, the One will be energetic and goal-oriented, while the Eight will be toler- ant, able to relate and respectful. Typically, the One will inspire decency and especially sensitivity in the relationship's external contacts, while the Eight will inspire the One to stick their neck out and come out of their comfort zone. The One will also contribute with structure, quality and depth, while the Eight will contribute by being the rock upon which the One can rely.

Both Types will contribute to the relationship with respect both for each other and for other people, and they have a particular respect for the consequences of their actions. Both fight for a higher cause – the One for the many, the Eight for the few, or for all those that the Eight might be able to influence. This focus on the "good deed" brings them closer to each other, and the cause is often more important than the relationship. Viewed from outside, the relationship is likely to be perceived as re- bellious and professional, dedicated, loving, tender, and focused upon good causes.

Description of the relationship when both partners feel under pressure

When the interaction is restrictive, accusatory, destructive and demo- tivating, the One will feel provoked by the rebellious streak in the Eight, who does not always follow the narrow path of virtue advocated by the One. Conversely, the Eight will ratchet up the provocation when the One begins to engage in sarcastic reprovals. Typically, the One will struggle to get the Eight to toe the line and behave themselves, while the Eight will perceive this as a form of control and therefore provoke even more.

The One will begin to distance him/herself from the Eight's insensi- tive, unethical and disrespectful ways and will begin to establish cardinal principles that should be respected by the Eight, such as being faithful to their spouse, treating their dog well, speaking with consideration about religious minorities or talking about competitors respectfully. Type 8 will feel controlled and dominated by Type 1's principles, and will attempt to find a way round the problem in order to remain in the relationship without feeling constrained.

Description of the measures that may bring the partners closer to each other

Both partners are strong-willed, stubborn and deeply attached to a sense of both anger and fair play. Type 1 feels that there are certain ways/prin- ciples upon which the relationship is built, while Type 8 needs to feel like a free bird without restrictions. This principle of freedom often leads the Eight to overstep the mark just to show the One that they are not judge and jury. Type 1s have a Frustration-relationship with the Protective Fig- ure, meaning that very early in life they had to foster a number of robust rules/principles around the way things work, including the way one is in a relationship. Type 8s have a Rejection-relationship with the Nurturing Figure, meaning that the Eight takes over the protective role. In other words, the Eight acts out the definitive Protective Figure externally, while the One has constructed the definitive internal Protective Figure. It is the conflict between these fundamental outer and inner Protective Figures that consumes the relationship's energy.

It is recommended that Type 1 works on his/her flexibility and curi- osity, and that Type 8 works on his/her humility and self-righteous, de- structive energy.

Relationship between Type 1 and Type 9

Description of the relationship when both partners feel resourceful

When the interaction is enriching, supportive, inspiring and evolving, the One will be sharp and precise, while the Nine will be inclusive and participatory. Typically, the One will bring out the more engaging side of the Nine, while the Nine will inspire stamina and tenacity. At the same time, the One will contribute with wisdom and profundity, while the Nine will contribute with robustness and stability.

Both Types will contribute with a mutual respect for each other's differences, such that the One does not take things so personally and the Nine dispenses with his/her passive aggression. They are not necessar- ily focussed on the relationship itself, but the One's principles and the Nine's stubbornness are toned down.

Viewed from outside, the relationship is likely to be perceived as stable, vibrant, balanced, predictable and sensible.

Description of the relationship when both partners feel under pressure

When the interaction is restrictive, accusatory, destructive and demoti- vating, the One will be frustrated by the Nine's ability to kick decisions into the long grass and the Nine's passive-aggressive approach to con- flict. The Nine will feel violated and overwhelmed by the One's quick opinions and decision-making. Ones have their principles to fight for, while Nines do not necessarily fight for anything – they are more likely not to fight for anything.

The Type 1 feels that (s)he is fighting for the relationship and feels that the Nine lacks the will to fight. Conversely, the Nine will struggle to avoid being overwhelmed and violated by the One, so they will have their fights, but with opposite signs (plus and minus) in the relationship. Type 1 has a tendency to take things personally, but in many ways there is nothing to be taken personally from the Nine. This rather flat feeling awakens a deep frustration within the One, who often considers putting his/her foot down in order to deal with some of the big issues in the relationship.

Description of the measures that may bring the partners closer to each other

In a way, this is a quiet relationship, in which the Nine absorbs the One's frustration, while over time the One begins to pick the right or essential confrontations with the Nine. The One has a Frustration-relationship with the Protective Figure, while the Nine has an Attachment-relation- ship with both Figures. This means that where the One has expectations and makes demands of the Nine, these are met with infinite latitude… which is mistaken for indifference by the One. The Nine's double Attach- ment-relationship means, in practice, the Nine has difficulty completely recognising the clarity of both roles, and when the One demands clari- ty around the protective qualities (but does not actually experience any clarity), this will often give rise to the challenges faced by the relation-ship.

It is recommended that Type 1 works on setting precise and realistic terms for the Nine's decision-making process, and that Type 9 works on finding the time to stand up for selected areas in the relationship.

Relationship between Type 2 and Type 2

Description of the relationship when both partners feel resourceful

When the interaction is enriching, supportive, inspiring and evolving, the Twos will be able to relate to each other, and be present, attentive, genuine and supportive of each other. They will give each other space, even as they challenge the other to stand on their own two feet.

They will both contribute to a relationship in which they bring out the best in the other and their nurturing qualities blossom. They will also challenge the other to realise their dreams and passions as well as to clearly express their needs and wants.

Viewed from outside, the relationship is likely to be perceived as caring, close, attentive, genuine, supportive, mentoring and understanding.

Description of the relationship when both partners feel under pressure

When the interaction is restrictive, accusatory, destructive and demotivating, both Twos will freeze the other out of the relationship, shut the other out, and be emotionally cold and manipulative. They will con- stantly encounter their own dark sides, because the other will be self-ab- sorbed, trapped in their own feelings, accusatory, judgemental and dramatic; they will also lose themselves in the role of victim and martyr. They will instil in the other the feeling of being cold and cynical, which is precisely what the Two fears in him/herself.

Description of the measures that may bring the partners closer to each other

Both Twos have a great need to be noticed, heard and accommodated by the other, and both require the other to acknowledge them first be- fore they are able to acknowledge the other. It is an impossible task for both to be fully acknowledged by the other first – before they can move on in the relationship – which simply means that each freezes the other out and hopes, with a streak of martyrdom, that the other can reconcile the partners. They both have a Frustration-relationship with the Protec- tive Figure and therefore can barely tolerate the other being cold and shutting down the relationship. Type 2 has, moreover, a need for phys- ical contact, but when both sides shut the other out, this also applies to physical contact; this remains with the Two, who has a tendency to bear grudges.

However, when the Two-couple succeed in evolving together, they will have worked through a substantial proportion of their essential (often traumatic) habits and patterns in connection with their Object Relation. In practice, this will mean that the Two will realise that it is not possible to be noticed, heard, and completely and optimally accommodated, and that their reaction in freezing others out, and therefore punishing them for not accommodating them 100 percent, does not help to accommo- date each other within the relationship.

It is recommended that the Twos work on expressing their needs clearly and accepting a "no", while investigating precisely how the Object Relation can be that place where they achieve the great breakthrough in their personal development.

Relationship between Type 2 and Type 3

Description of the relationship when both partners feel resourceful

When the interaction is enriching, supportive, inspiring and evolving, the Two will be emotional and expressive, while the Three will be sincere and able to relate to the Two. Typically, the Two will bring out an ability within the Three to get in touch with their own heart or feelings, while the Three will inspire the Two to share their human gifts more broadly with the rest of the world. The Two will also contribute with compassion and an interest in others, while the Three will contribute with self-worth and direction.

Both Types will contribute with an interest in humanity and in each other, and will focus on what is valued within the relationship. This fo- cus on the relationship is concerned with being there for each other, ac- knowledging and accommodating each other and bringing out the best in each other.

Viewed from outside, the relationship is likely to be perceived as vital and rewarding, enterprising and dynamic, as well as humane and per- sonal.

Description of the relationship when both partners feel under pressure

When the interaction is restrictive, accusatory, destructive and demo- tivating, the Two will feel that the Three is too busy, that everything be- comes a project, and that the Two is just a resource in the Three's life. Conversely, the Three will feel that the highly emotional discussions are too long-winded, meaningless and endless, and that the Two's demands to be fully accommodated and understood (even in pressurised situations) become difficult to honour for the busy Three. Twos will sacrifice themselves for their relationships and stretch themselves to unburden the Three as much as possible with the hope that this will free up time for the relationship. However, the extra time that the Two can create for the Three is often simply filled with new projects. Threes have a tendency to throw themselves into all their projects with the excuse that they will also benefit the Two's life. They will therefore feel they both sacrifice them- selves for the relationship; however, both do so for the wrong reasons.

Description of the measures that may bring the partners closer to each other

Both partners will sacrifice themselves, each in their own way, and nei- ther of them will acknowledge or work out the other's way of sacrificing themselves. Type 2s sacrifice themselves to get acknowledgement (or a stronger relationship/greater intimacy) from the Three, while Threes sacrifice themselves to create possibilities for the relationship (family). Type 2 has a Rejection-relationship with the Protective Figure, which means that the Type 2 can become afraid when the Three is too harsh, determined or resolute around topics concerned with the relationship. Type 3 has an Attachment-relationship with the Nurturing Figure and therefore has a diffuse or ambivalent attitude toward the relationship with the qualities that the Nurturing Figure represents, and which are precisely the qualities that the Two has focussed on and developed to perfection. It often happens that the Two expects that the Three can sup- ply just as intimate and sympathetic a presence as the Two him/herself can.

It is recommended that the Type 2 works at contributing to the rela- tionship (sacrificing themselves) for the right reason and that the Three works at discovering when they use the Two as a resource.

Relationship between Type 2 and Type 4

Description of the relationship when both partners feel resourceful

When the interaction is enriching, supportive, inspiring and evolving, the Two will be practical and sympathetic, while the Four will be realistic and supportive. Typically, the Two will bring out the more practical and creative side of the Four, while the Four will inspire both greater depth and lightness. At the same time, the Two will bring warm-heartedness to the relationship, while the Four contributes with useful human insights. Both partners will contribute with warmth, care, depth and humanity, which over time forges close bonds, incorporating all forms of emotional fallout, disappointments, highlights and stability. Considerable attention is paid to the relationship, and together they are able to lose themselves in the moment and whatever arises during the associated conversation. Viewed from outside, the relationship is likely to be perceived as essential, deep, emotional, tender, humane and open to learning.

Description of the relationship when both partners feel under pressure

When the interaction is restrictive, accusatory, destructive and demotivating, the Two will react strongly when the Four is "impossible" or freez- es them out within the relationship. Exactly this "freezing out" of the relationship is the Two's preferred act of punishment, but it is regarded as intolerable when the Four does the same. Conversely, the Four will be overwhelmed when the Two "steals" the emotional space that the Four intends to commandeer. Type 2s also need to be recognised, but this is more to do with the Two having to acknowledge the Four and accept   or accommodate all forms of Four's behaviour. They thus have mutual wishes or demands of each other, which in many cases are never ful-filled, so the relationship may evolve into something enormously stable and robust...while also involving a great deal of discord and many dis-appointments, misunderstandings and shutouts within the relationship.

Description of the measures that may bring the partners closer together

Both partners, then, have a tendency to steal the demands of the other and turn these demands against each other. It is, of course, impossible for both parties to secure these demands from the other, but when they appreciate the nature of their tacit game of expectations, the relation-ship will begin to evolve. Type 2 has a Rejection-relationship with the Protective Figure, meaning that tiny breakdowns in the relationship are difficult for the Two to deal with. Type 4 has a Frustration-relationship with both Figures, with the result that the demands made of the Two by the Four can never be redeemed. We can say that the Two's "strongest" defence for being disappointed is to freeze out the other within the re-lationship, which leads to dramas and accusations from the Four...and hence to the Two shutting out the Four even more.

It is recommended that Type 2 works on understanding the negative effects of his/her retaliatory shut-outs and that Type 4 works on breaking free from his/her accusatory approach to the Two.

Relationship between Type 2 and Type 5

Description of the relationship when both parties feel resourceful

When the interaction is enriching, supportive, inspiring and evolving, the Two will be welcoming and tender, while the Five will be deep and able to relate to the other. Typically, the Two will bring out the character of the Five, while the Five will inspire the Two to examine things more closely. The Two will also contribute to the relationship with respect, lat- itude and understanding, while the Five will contribute with existential precision and practical wisdom.

Both Types will contribute to a relationship in which there is respect for each other's "fragility" or eccentricities, and, over time, the relation- ship will build upon strong foundations such that both feel noticed, heard and accommodated.

The relationship will not necessarily be highly energetic, but together they will be able to make decisions and deal with things as necessary.

Viewed from the outside, the relationship is likely to be perceived as solid, caring, affectionate, respectful and one in which the partners sup- port each other.

Description of the relationship when both partners feel under pressure

When the interaction is restrictive, accusatory, destructive and demoti- vating, the Two will feel unappreciated, unimportant and insignificant due to the Five's difficulties with relating to others and opening him/ herself up. Type 2 has a tendency to shut out the Five as a type of punish- ment, but this has no impact on the Five, who simply shrugs, implying that the Two is too childish, primitive and incompetent to waste time on.

Type 5 becomes frustrated by the Two's dramatization, self-absorption and constant demands on the relationship, as well as his/her need to do things together and to be connected.

Type 2s will often feel that they are in a relationship with an empty vessel without emotion, energy or vital signs and whose batteries have gone flat. This engenders feelings of anger and impotence that merge into manipulation, which the Five simply downplays or ignores. Type 5s will often have the sense that they are being misused or that they must provide something special to the Two just to have a "sensible" or "re- warding" conversation, thus making the Five shut down even more.

Description of the measures that may bring the partners closer to each other

Both partners have a strong tendency to reject the other and to shut out each other in the relationship to the extent that the other no longer mat- ters to them. Type 2 shuts down in order to discipline the Five into ac- tion, while the Five simply doubles down such that they can neither feel anything for, or relate to, the Two any longer. Type 2 has a Rejection-re- lationship with the Protective Figure, while the Five has a Rejection-re- lationship with both Figures. These unequivocal rejections entail both partners attempting to be the one that rejects the other before they are themselves rejected.

It is recommended that Type 2 works on objectivity and that Type 5 works on explaining how they are feeling.

Relationship between Type 2 and Type 6

Description of the relationship when both partners feel resourceful

When the interaction is enriching, supportive, inspiring and evolving, the Two will be both supportive and challenging, while the Six will be instructive and collaborative. Typically, the Two will bring out the calm side of the Six, while the Six will inspire the Two to fight for his/her values. The Two will also contribute to the relationship with factual, authen- tic conversation, while the Six will contribute with sensitive leadership.

Both Types will be loyal and supportive toward each other, while also lavishing care and attention on the relationship itself. This internal fo- cus may foster an extraordinary strength, overcoming many challenges, although it can also get a little out of hand, shifting attention away from other important aspects of life.

Viewed from the outside, the relationship is likely to be perceived as caring, loving, stable, intense, trusting and unified.

Description of the relationship when both partners feel under pressure

When the interaction is restrictive, accusatory, destructive and demoti- vating, the Two will feel manipulated by the Six's attempts to find their place within the relationship by challenging the Two. Conversely, the Six will also feel manipulated by the Two's constant need for appreciation and to be heard in a special way. Type 2 will play the role of victim or martyr to get the Six to behave in a particular way, while the Six deploys insoluble riddles to test the Two's resolve. An example of this might be that, during an argument, the Six runs into the garden to see what hap- pens; if the Two hurries out to check up on the Six, the former is superficial, but if the Six waits too long before coming into the garden...well, the Two is insufficiently engaged. Twos are happy to deploy such methods, but are highly resistant to their deployment against them.

Description of the measures that may bring the partners closer together

Both partners are extremely focussed on the relationship, although the Two mainly concentrates on togetherness or symbiosis with the Six, while the Six is more concerned with being there for each other and demonstrating loyalty. The Two therefore sees the individuals in the re- lationship, while the Six sees the relationship as a whole. Type 2s have a Rejection-relationship with the Protective Figure and therefore find it difficult that the Six sometimes exhibits the protective qualities and sometimes absolutely does not exhibit them. Type 6s have an Attach- ment-relationship to the Protective Figure and therefore demand that the Two is the one who unambiguously demonstrates the protective qualities – at least for themselves and in their own lives.

It is recommended that Type 2 works on clearly expressing his/her needs and that Type 6 works on being more specific in his/her expecta- tions.

Relationship between Type 2 and Type 7

Description of the relationship when both partners feel resourceful

When the interaction is enriching, supportive, inspiring and evolving, the Two will feel vibrant and optimistic, while the Seven will display gratefulness and empathy. Typically, the Two will bring the human side out of the Seven, while the Seven will inspire light-heartedness and re- alism.

Both Types will contribute to a relationship in which they will stand up for each other and quickly get over breakdowns or misunderstand- ings. They will both work together to get the best out of the relationship, and each has their own way of encouraging or cheering up the other.

Viewed from outside, the relationship is likely to be perceived as vi- brant, optimistic, generous, supportive and appreciative.

Description of the relationship when both partners feel under pressure

When the interaction is restrictive, accusatory, destructive and demoti- vating, the Two will feel anger and disillusionment over the Seven's in- difference toward the crucial subjects the Two would like to discuss. The Seven, on the other hand, will feel despairing and disappointed, and will try to find ways to distract them both, which will merely make the Two even more annoyed. The Seven has a sharp and sarcastic tongue, striking at the heart of the Two, who attempts to defend him/herself with threats and repudiations, which just makes the Seven even less bothered about the relationship.

The Two will invest in the relationship, while the Seven will invest in projects, work or adventures. The Seven will often attempt to escape "negative" feelings, while to some extent the Two lives to experience them. There can therefore be a tendency for the Two to demand that the Seven sits still and listens to both the Seven's own and to the Two's feel- ings. As a rule, this will generate even more frustration, and the Seven's temperament will ensure that the experiment will never be repeated.

Description of the measures that may bring the partners closer together

Both partners want the relationship to be rewarding and positive, and the Two works to ensure that attentiveness and vibrancy in the relation- ship does indeed generate rewards and positivity. Type 7 works to gen- erate liveliness, happiness and positive energy through activities. This approach, however, can seem remote for the Two, who might initially participate in these activities but eventually finds them hollow or emp- ty. Type 2 has a Rejection-relationship with the Protective Figure, which means that, when the Seven is all too "protective", the Two will withdraw. Type 7 has a Frustration-relationship with the Nurturing Figure, mean- ing that at heart the Seven longs for precisely what is offered by the Two as "representative" of the Nurturing Figure.

It is recommended that Type 2 works on establishing clear expecta- tions rather than punishments, and that Type 7 works on reaching out to meet the Two in his/her feelings.

Relationship between Type 2 and Type 8

Description of the relationship when both partners feel resourceful

When the interaction is enriching, supportive, inspiring and evolving, the Two will be energetic and have a pride that comes from within, while the Eight will be gentle, open and cautious. Typically, the Two will bring out the Eight's more genuine side, such that nothing is forced or negoti- ated within the relationship, while the Eight will inspire the Two to say "yes" and "no" to the important decisions in life and to make his/her feelings clear. The Two will also contribute to the relationship with a gen- uine interest for the other and for people outside the relationship, while the Eight will contribute with courage and unadorned love, and by chal- lenging habits and frameworks.

Both Types will be concerned with fairness and respect for the rela- tionship and whatever the other (and people outside the relationship) has to offer. The relationship's combination of strength and love, of cour- age and vulnerability, of ambition and humility creates a special rela- tionship capable of withstanding a great many challenges on a daily ba- sis.

Viewed from outside, the relationship is likely to be perceived as har- monious, stable, vital, loving and nurturing.

Description of the relationship when both partners feel under pressure

When the interaction is restrictive, accusatory, destructive and demoti- vating, the Two will feel pressurised, used and ignored in the face of the Eight's self-absorption and self-centredness. Conversely, the Eight will feel repelled by the weakness, subservience and victimhood displayed by the Two when a pressurised situation arises. They are both experts in freezing the other out of the relationship – to the extent that they can frighten themselves over how cold and harsh they can be to each other.

Type 2s will often feel that they sacrifice themselves to make things work in the relationship and have therefore saved something in the "relationship bank". Meanwhile, the Two finds it difficult to say "no" to the Eight and to express his/her needs and wants directly. However, this indirect approach is difficult for the Eight to deal with, so the latter has a tendency to pressurise the Two into taking a position one way or another – including about the Eight him/herself.

Description of the measures that may bring the partners closer to each other

As mentioned above, both partners are experts at shutting the other out, given that the Two feels taken for granted and the Eight feels repulsed by the Two's weakness. In many ways, exactly this Type-couple are opposites, in that the Two has a Rejection-relationship with the Protective Figure, while the Eight has a Rejection-relationship with the Nurturing Figure. This means that the Two has never learned to say "no", take a position, or express his/her wants and needs – but the Eight *has* done so. Conversely, the Eight has never learned to delve into the feelings of others, to get involved in others' difficult emotions, or to "go the extra mile" to make a relationship work—but the Two *has* done so. When times are good, this pair-type is able to draw upon each other's skills; in hard times, however, each takes the view that they hold the key to changing the other's habits, but they have frozen the other out of the relationship... and the valuable "relationship key" can no longer be passed on.

It is recommended that Type 2 works on expressing his/her needs clearly, as well as learning how to say "no" in a non-dismissive way, while Type 8 should work on accessing the Two's emotional universe without also making demands about how the Two should feel, think or behave.

Notes on a romantic relationship

In a romantic relationship, a fundamental demand of the Type 2 will be that (s)he is fully noticed, heard and accommodated – and this is ex- tremely challenging for their partner. The Two will have a sense that if their partner really loves them, their partner will also know how the Two would like to receive appreciation, love, care, attention and presence. Yet the Two will also feel secure enough to be lost, self-denying, depressed, gloomy and self-deprecating, requiring that their partner is there for them and can embrace their self-destructive and gloomy perspective.

In a romantic relationship, Type 8s will fundamentally demand trust and loyalty, while also revealing themselves, their weaknesses and hu- mility to their partner in the hope that their partner will do the same for them. They will attempt to take over and be impossible to be with, to test whether their partner will still be there for them. Yet the Eight will feel secure enough to moan, to be weak, hurt, exhausted, indecisive and flat, which, in itself, is a provocative way for the Eight to behave, requiring the partner to tolerate their whining and victimhood.

In relation to the Eight, the Two will require enormous empathy, un- derstanding and tolerance, which the Eight will react against, as it is ex- actly these qualities that the Eight is averse to and that reflect the Eight's own behaviour in a romantic relationship. To see him/herself mirrored, or to see the other take the weak role, is in itself a provocation for the Eight.

In relation to Type 2, the Eight will be more onerous and strident than normal, while also demanding that the Two cope with the Eight's moan- ing and complaining, particularly because it is usually the Two who takes refuge in a relationship by being "small and vulnerable" and needs to have their hand held. So the Two will experience the Eight's behaviour as an additional pressure, almost as though they have an extra child in the family that they must take care of.

Relationship between Type 2 and Type 9

Description of the relationship when both partners feel resourceful

When the interaction is enriching, supportive, inspiring and evolving, the Two will be visible in a supportive way, while the Nine will be communicative and able to relate to the Two. Typically, the Two will bring out the more outgoing side of the Nine, while the Nine will inspire the Two to let his/her feelings go, so the Two does not get trapped in his/her feelings.

Both Types will contribute to an inclusive and understanding relationship, in which there is space for both partners and where both can "mess about" in their own way without the other becoming too provoked. This lightness in the relationship will be a strength in the long run, although over time a lack of focus on other aspects of life, such as work, hobbies, career, projects and finance, can arise.

Viewed from outside, the relationship is likely to seem gentle, inclusive, understanding, friendly and humane.

Description of the relationship when both partners feel under pressure

When the interaction is limiting, accusatory, destructive and demoti- vating, the Two will attempt to push the Nine into expressing their feel- ings and will be particularly happy when the Nine displays dissatisfac- tion – including with the relationship itself. For the Two, it is important to have something to work with in a purely emotional sense within the relationship, while the Nine simply hopes that the Two's demands will just disappear by themselves and that the difficult times will pass all by themselves.

Type 2s thus feel that they struggle and toil in order to build a relationship with the Nine, but they are slow to anger and rarely fight with the Nine. The Nine idles through life with the Two as support, and only in situations where the Two is too "rough" or unreasonable will they raise their voice and speak in clear terms.

Description of the measures that may bring the partners closer to each other

Both partners would like to enjoy a secure and stable relationship but work on this project in very different ways. What is special about this relationship is that the Two is not provoked by the protective reaction from the Nine because this is seldom provided. This "nothingness" or passivity in the relationship can make the Two insecure, but the edge is quickly taken from this insecurity by the Two's calm disposition. Type 2 has a Rejection-relationship with the Protective Figure, which normally causes problems when the other is too protective/instructive in a way perceived by the Two as threatening. Type 2 has a Rejection-relationship with both Figures, which means that the Nine has difficulty in recognis- ing the qualities in both Figures and therefore in expressing them to the Two. Given time, however, the Two can become a guide for the Nine, who may therefore establish a deeper contact with both qualities and strengthen the Two in the relationship.

It is recommended that the Type 2 works on providing clear instructions and expectations, and that Type 9 works on bringing out his/her character and dares to reveal his/her personality more (which the Two would love).

Relationship between Type 3 and Type 3

Description of the relationship when both partners feel resourceful

When the interaction is enriching, supportive, inspiring and evolving, the two Threes will be energetic, original and authentic. They will both contribute to a relationship in which they bring out value-creation in the other. Here, "value-creation" should be understood to mean that they act and bring about change, and what they create has value for others. They will be continually reminding each other of what is true and right, and they will also be each other's best cheerleader.

They will both contribute to a relationship in which something is created and built, while there is still space to talk about such subjects as loneliness, self-worth and self-deception. There will probably also be space for personal development, which might become an "indoor sport", as something that should be displayed, or a more long-term process, cre- ating a common mind-set in both of them.

Viewed from outside, the relationship is likely to be perceived as effective, goal-oriented, energetic, active, sincere, rewarding and satisfying.

Description of the relationship when both partners feel under pressure

When the interaction is restrictive, accusatory, destructive and demotivat- ing, both Threes will be frustrated that the other fails to follow the right principles and that the other so obviously takes the wrong decisions. They will constantly encounter their own dark side, because the other will be too narrow-minded, rigid in their principles, inflexible, myopic, closed and self-righteous. They will instil in the other a feeling of being wrong, slapdash or irresponsible, which is exactly what Threes fear in themselves.

Description of the measures that may bring the partners closer to each

Both Threes have their own lofty principles about how to be in the relationship with each other, and both work hard to ensure that the partner understands and lives up to these principles. Of course, this is an impossible task, and when they start being critical and accusatory toward each other, the response is equally critical and accusatory. They both have a Frustration-relationship with the Protective Figure and attempt to introduce principles and rules into the relationship to get it to function. At the same time, however, Threes identify with their own rules, so this requires them to soften the rules and principles at the core of their identity, which is an extremely difficult thing to do. However, when the Three-couple do succeed in evolving together, they will have worked through a substan- tial proportion of their essential (often traumatic) habits and patterns in connection with their Object Relation. In practice, this will mean that the Three will figure out that the world is not wrong and that it is not their job to fix things so that they are right and proper.

It is recommended that they work on developing flexibility and curiosity and on investigating precisely how the Object Relation can be that place where they achieve the great breakthrough in their personal development.

Relationship between Type 3 and Type 4

Description of the relationship when both partners feel resourceful

When the interaction is enriching, supportive, inspiring and evolving, the Three will be open and able to relate to the other, while the Four will be practical and motivated. Typically, the Three will bring out the more disciplined side of the Four, while the Four will inspire originality and beauty (in its broadest sense). The Three will contribute to the relation- ship with realism and energy, while the Four will contribute aestheti- cism, depth and character.

Both Types will focus on the essential and the practical, such that these provide energy to both partners in their own way. They will also chal- lenge each other in a caring way and bring out the original and authentic in each other. Thus, they will focus on their internal qualities, but mainly because they wish to bring the internal out into the external world. The Three will be more personal in his/her outlook, while the Four will be more practical and durable.

Viewed from outside, the relationship is likely to be perceived to be original, able to relate, team-oriented, practical, functional, intense, and challenging in a mutually caring way.

Description of the relationship when both partners feel under pressure

When the interaction is restrictive, accusatory, destructive and demo- tivating, the Three will react to the Four's drawn-out emotional antics by, at first, keeping their frustrations and feelings hidden. Later, the Three will try to work out a practical solution to the Four's "problem", and will finally go their own way, leaving the Four to their own "decline", as the Three sees it. Conversely, the Four will feel violated, criticised and crushed by the Three's "know-it-all" attitude, practical ingenuity and dedicated vigour.

Type 3 will work on the practical aspect of the relationship and go into "fix mode" every time the Four wishes to share their experiences (especially their inner experiences) with the Three. The Four will try to find a place for his/her feelings in the Three's project-oriented approach to daily life and the relationship's challenges. Type 3 criticises through body language and attitudes, while the Four criticises both directly and through indirect, raw hints.

Description of the measures that may bring the partners closer together

Both partners are intensely concerned about their own worth and do not take criticism or feedback particularly well. Type 3s take criticism personally and feel that they cannot be themselves, while Fours can also take criticism personally and are just reminded of their own inter- nal critic (tending in certain cases toward self-hatred). Type 3s have an Attachment-relationship with the Nurturing Figure and therefore find it difficult to deal with Four's feelings, their need to be acknowledged and their deep desire for a close, attentive relationship – because this is pre- cisely what Threes themselves desire. Type 4 has a Frustration-relation- ship with both Figures and therefore creates an impossible situation for the Three to live up to, as in practice the Three should be able to supply all the qualities represented by the two Figures.

It is recommended that Type 3 works on his/her "know-it-all" attitude, and that Type 4 works on his/her criticism of the Three – particularly of the Three's identity.

Relationship between Type 3 and Type 5

Description of the relationship when both partners feel resourceful

When the interaction is enriching, supportive, inspiring and evolving, the Three will be inviting and playful, while the Five will be realistic and able to relate. Typically, the Three will bring out the more productive and playful side of the Five, while the Five will inspire depth and an objective approach to halting unviable projects. At the same time, the Three will contribute to the relationship with originality and resolve, while the Five will contribute with thoughtfulness and vulnerability.

Both Types will contribute with practical care, focussing on each other's inner universe. This focus on the inner universe is mutually support- ive and inspirational, making it possible for both of them to relate to the outside world in a more understanding and practical way.

Viewed from outside, the relationship is likely to be perceived as practical, respectful, cheerful, soothing and mutually acknowledging.

Description of the relationship when both partners feel under pressure

When the interaction is restrictive, accusatory, destructive and demoralising, the Three will be frustrated over the longevity of the Five's suffering, their interminable explanations, abstract solutions and expectant attention. Conversely, the Five will reject Three's all-too-rapid tempo and conclusions, and will quickly judge them to be shallow and lacking in seriousness.

Type 3 will have a lot of good advice for the Five, which the Five naturally cannot accept, while, conversely, the Five has a lot of solutions for the Three, which the Three is equally unable to accept. Type 3s shut out this good advice because they feel that their intellect is being talked down, while Fives shut it out because they think that the Three does not know what (s)he is talking about.

Description of the measures that may bring the partners closer to each other

Both partners have a strong tendency to feel more knowledgeable than the other, and disagreements can arise as to who sees things more accu- rately, who is in possession of the truth, or who has found the best solu- tion to a problem. This can result in the partners not really talking to each other, but more commenting on each other's comments. Type 3 has an Attachment-relationship with the Nurturing Figure, meaning that they can have challenges with respecting, relating to or bonding with the Five, while they also require the Five to completely acknowledge them and not change them. Type 5 has a Rejection-relationship with both Figures, meaning that they have difficulty relating emotionally to the Three, while they do not really know how they should set boundaries for the Three and therefore end up doing so too resolutely or determinedly.

It is recommended that the Type 3 works on his/her patience and de- sire to "show the way" to the Five, and that the Type 5 works on being precise in expressing his/her wishes to the Three.

Relationship between Type 3 and Type 6

Description of the relationship when both partners feel resourceful

When the interaction is enriching, supportive, inspiring and evolving, the Three will be inviting and challenging, while the Six will offer guid- ance and indulgence. Typically, the Three will bring out a lighter, more mischievous side of the Six, while the Six will inspire loyalty and a desire to learn. At the same time, the Three will contribute to a more rebellious relationship in which things are not taken for granted, while the Six will contribute with stability and rigour.

Both Types will contribute to a warm, vigorous and playful relation- ship, where the focus is outside themselves. Thus there is greater focus on tasks, projects or activities, and when, once in a while, the conversa- tion turns personal or private, it does so with the highest mutual respect, attentiveness and care.

Viewed from outside, the relationship is likely to be perceived as prac- tical, rational, respectful, loyal, playful and routine-filled.

Description of the relationship when both partners feel under pressure

When the interaction is restrictive, accusatory, destructive and demoti- vating, the Three will feel that the Six is problematizing things too much, that they are criticising or that they are reactionary. Conversely, the Six will feel insecure with the Three, bordering on a sense of betrayal.

Type 3 invests a great deal of energy in the relationship by offering good advice and getting things started for the Six, while the Six invests a great deal of energy in the relationship by building structures and pro- cesses. Neither of these approaches works for the other, and, as both believe that mind-reading is possible, that they take too much for granted often creates problems for this relationship.

Description of the measures that may bring the partners closer to each other

In this relationship, both partners believe that they are the adult in the relationship, and that it is they who have worked out how things should be done. At the same time, both parties are extremely sensitive about being reproached, which they take as sharp criticism. Type 3 has an At- tachment-relationship with the Nurturing Figure, which means that the Three can find it difficult to show their full care for, and understanding of, the Six. Type 6 has an Attachment-relationship with the Protective Figure, which means, in turn, that they find it difficult to set boundaries for the Three, to understand when the Three sets boundaries, or to feel secure in the Three's company.

It is recommended that Type 3 works on his/her relationship to care and loyalty, and that Type 6 works on his/her relationship to self-man- agement.

Relationship between Type 3 and Type 7

Description of the relationship when both partners feel resourceful

When the interaction is enriching, supportive, inspiring and evolving, the Three will be practical and focussed, while the Seven will be encour- aging and able to relate. Typically, the Three will bring the more practical and disciplined side out of the Seven, while the Seven will inspire the other to throw themselves into activities and to see themselves in a pos- itive light. At the same time, the Three will contribute to them following their heart and to probing more deeply than the Seven would tradition- ally wish, while the Seven will contribute with an impulse to discover the magical, positive and generous aspects of the Three. Both Types have a lot of energy and creativity, and they will contribute to a relationship in which things get started and they are not afraid to throw themselves into activities together. Their special relationship with the Nurturing Figure will result in a profound and respectful partnership that values and re- spects their differences. They will want to start up activities and projects together which have value for those close to them and for the next gen- eration.

Viewed from outside, the relationship is likely to be perceived as ded- icated, practical, unafraid to act, having a love of learning, and which is problem-solving, loving and respectful.

Description of the relationship when both parties feel under pressure

When the interaction is restrictive, accusatory, destructive and demoti- vating, the Three will feel exasperated by the Seven's inconsistency, lack of planning, forgetfulness, spontaneity and "whatever" attitude. Conversely, the Seven will become tired and frustrated by the Three's practical approach to things – and will always want to disrupt the plans and processes undertaken by the Three to keep the Seven under control.

Type 3 will feel that (s)he is the adult in the relationship and will be- gin to look down on Seven's clearly childish approach to life and what is important within it. Type 7, however, is quite capable of standing up for him/herself by resorting to cutting sarcasm and biting irony, which is taken as personal criticism by the Three, who therefore slowly begins to freeze out the Seven – while the latter merely shrugs his/her shoulders at the Three shutting down the relationship.

Description of the measures that may bring the partners closer to each other

Both partners in the relationship have a great deal of energy, are cre- ative and have a "can do" attitude. In principle, they can function fine without the other, which often tends to happen in these relationships if they do not have the time, will or ability to get to grips with their relation- ship. Type 3 has an Attachment-relationship with the Nurturing Figure, while Type 7 has a Frustration-relationship with the Nurturing Figure. This combination means that they both want (demand) the other par- ty to be the one that first shows understanding, care, trust, acceptance and latitude toward themselves. As this can never happen, their mutual breakthrough first takes place when they begin to put themselves in the other's shoes.

It is recommended that Type 3 works on his/her condescending and "know-it-all" attitude toward the Seven, while Type 7 works on under- standing how sarcasm and criticism are corrosive for the Three.

Relationship between Type 3 and Type 8

Description of the relationship when both partners feel resourceful

When the relationship is enriching, supportive, destructive and evolving, the Three will be dedicated and original, while the Eight will be construc- tive and gentle. Typically, the Three will bring the more original and creative side out of the Eight, while the Eight will inspire the Three to deal with the necessary conflicts while the Three has a relationship with those the con- flict is about. Moreover, the Three will contribute to the relationship with passionate ambition, inventiveness and value-creation, while the Eight will contribute to it with doggedness, humility and a robust authenticity.

Both Types will contribute to a shared, powerful energy, the basic foundation of which consists of their own values, human relationships and their empathic behaviour. They will focus on their tasks, their ability to act, and on making progress. Together they will be a team that encour- ages both partners.

Viewed from outside, the relationship is likely to be perceived as hard-working, professional, ambitious, respectful, dedicated and un- stoppable.

Description of the relationship when both partners feel under pressure

When the relationship is restrictive, accusatory, destructive and demoti-vating, the Three will feel overwhelmed, violated and threatened by the Eight's energy and anger. Conversely, the Eight will feel powerless when (in his/her view) the Three finds quick and easy solutions and moves the goalposts or changes the terms by which objectives are deemed to be fulfilled. Typically, the Three will try to be "quick-smart", while the Eight will be forceful in enforcing his/her rights.

Type 3s will often feel that they must be the tolerant and flexible par- ty in the relationship – and will therefore feel at some point that they should be rewarded for their tolerance in the face of Eight's threats and provocations. Type 8s exert themselves physically and can feel the phys- ical consequences of working harder than the Three, so they will often demand that the Three works even harder – or acknowledges the Eight's extraordinary contribution to the relationship.

Description of the measures that may bring both partners closer to each other

Both parties have a marked tendency to place themselves in the centre of events, and in pressure situations both need the other to credit them before conflict resolution can begin to take place. At the same time, both close down the relationship and are equally stubborn and cold toward the other. Type 3s feel that they have been flexible, and have shown lat- itude and tolerance, but that there has to be a limit, while Type 8s feel that they are the only party contributing anything. At the same time, the Three may threaten the Eight's position within the hierarchy, while the Eight may start rumours about the Three, potentially damaging the lat- ter's image. Both Types have a special relationship with the Nurturing Figure, such that the Three is ambivalent about the relationship and has difficulties with it when things become intense, provocative or threaten- ing, while the Eight has a Rejection-relationship with the Nurturing Fig- ure, which means that a shutting out or rejection of the Three becomes massive, consistent and inflexible. While the Three flees the intensity, the Eight toils even more, so this relationship needs to refocus on the deeper value of being in the relationship.

It is recommended that Type 3 works on re-establishing contact with their heart while standing by or stepping back from their values, and, likewise, the Eight should work on re-establishing contact with their heart to bring out their compassion and forgiveness for themselves and for the Three.

Relationship between Type 3 and Type 9

Description of the relationship when both partners feel resourceful

When the interaction is enriching, supportive, inspiring and evolving, the Three will bring out the more productive and original side of the Nine, while the Nine will inspire sincerity and depth. The Three will also contribute to a relationship with events, adventures and opportunities, while the Nine will contribute with physical serenity and stability.

Both Types will contribute to a relationship in which personal development is a priority, and they have a sharper focus on internal, rather than external, success. They will build up a sense that they need each other and slowly construct a little tribe for themselves – particularly if there are children in the relationship.

Viewed from outside, the relationship is likely to be perceived as loving, stable, sensitive, physical, enduring and durable.

Description of the relationship when both partners feel under pressure

When the interaction is restrictive, accusatory, destructive and demotivating, the Three will feel confined or slowed down by the Nine and want to take matters a little more into their own hands. Conversely, the Nine will feel violated by the Three's need for quick comments on or re- sponses to things. Type 3s have a tendency to compare themselves to the outside world and will also do this within the relationship; they will also need areas in which they are the best or are masterful, while Type 9s tend to demonstrate indifference to essential issues – right to the point when they are forced to make a decision.

Type 3 will feel that their energy and vigour helps bring opportunities to the relationship, while the Nine will feel that they are the glue in the relationship. They therefore each have their own ideas about what is necessary in the relationship, but these ideas are not as a rule consistent with each other.

Description of the measures that may bring the partners closer to each other

Both have a tendency to feel that they put in more effort than the other, or that they put in a lot of effort that is unappreciated by the other. Type 3 has an Attachment-relationship with the Nurturing Figure, while the Nine has an Attachment-relationship with both Figures. This ambivalent and diffuse relationship finds its particular expression in the romantic aspect of the relationship, where both are compelled to surrender to their intuitions and, to some extent, shut down their thoughts and feel- ings. They have great unspoken expectations about how love grows and is maintained, but both of them should invest a little time introducing the other to their respective expectations. Moreover, they both have a tendency to believe that mind-reading is possible, meaning that they of- ten take their own interpretations for granted.

It is recommended that Type 3 works on showing physical attentive-ness and that Type 9 works on balancing the role of supporter with that of being supported.

Relationship between Type 4 and Type 4

Description of the relationship when both partners feel resourceful

When the interaction is enriching, supportive, inspiring and evolving, the two Fours will feel deeply confident in each other and bring out the most personal and human aspects of each other. They will both contrib- ute to a relationship in which they will gently challenge each other in practical and disciplined ways, will recognise in each other qualities pre- viously unnoticed, and will develop that person both want to be – both individually and within the relationship.

They will both contribute to a relationship in which the priority is complete self-realisation and in which both encourage each other to engage with deep and difficult feelings, while allowing these feelings to flow without leaving any aftermath. They will assist each other in dealing with both true and false feelings.

Viewed from outside, this relationship is likely to be regarded as emo- tional, dramatic, vigorous, challenging, vulnerable, human, original, au- thentic and with an aesthetic for life.

Description of the relationship when both partners feel under pressure

When the interaction is restrictive, accusatory, destructive and demo- tivating, both Fours will be frustrated that they are never afforded suffi- cient space, accommodated in the right way, listened to or allowed to be themselves in all aspects. They will constantly encounter their own dark sides, because the other will be too practical, banal, firm in their princi- ples, dull, unoriginal, simple, vulgar, emotionless, objective, cold, inflex- ible, inhumane, soulless and lacking aesthetic values. They will instil in the other a sense of being banal, unoriginal and empty from a human and emotional perspective – things that are precisely what the Four fears in him/herself.

Description of the measures that may bring the partners closer together

Both Fours have a deep connection to their inner universe – and thereby their own feelings – and use their partner as a wall against which they can bounce their feelings. This is, however, confusing to both of them be- cause they assume that they will get back a response to the feelings they convey to the world, but what actually comes back are just completely new feelings from the other Four – which are not related to the feelings originally conveyed, but simply fill the relationship with new demands to be heard. They both have a Frustration-relationship with both Fig- ures, meaning that they both want to be fully noticed and heard by the other, while the other must also supply direction and discipline for both of them. At the same time, the Four identifies with his/her feelings and therefore finds it extremely difficult not to believe that their feelings are true and that they ought to act on them.

However, when the Four-couple do succeed in evolving together, they will have worked through a substantial proportion of their (often trau- matic) essential habits and patterns in connection with their Object Re- lation. In practice, this will mean that the Four will figure out that they are already complete, unique and beautiful without doing anything at all to be so. Through self-acceptance, the Four comes to experience their breakthrough in their personal development and the double-relation- ship has the potential for such a breakthrough.

It is recommended that the Fours work on developing a deeper ac- ceptance of who or what they are and on investigating precisely how the Object Relation can be that place where they achieve the great break- through in their personal development.

Relationship between Type 4 and Type 5

Description of the relationship when both partners feel resourceful

When the interaction is enriching, supportive, inspiring and evolving, the Four will be inclusive and understanding, while the Five will be sin- cere and able to relate to the other. Typically, the Four will bring the more personal or natural side out of the Five, while the Five will contribute with precision and realism. At the same time, the Four will contribute to the relationship with appreciation and personal depth, while the Five will contribute with clarity and wisdom. Both Types will contribute with the essential and the undefinable (for example, beauty, wisdom, truth, presence, love), and have a deep respect for the diverse inner universe which both parties have to offer. This inner focus, combined with mutu- al respect and appreciation, can create a relationship that collaborates around the essential, but which has less interest in the external world. This Four-Five combination is, however, capable of supporting one other in their manifestation in the outside world.

Viewed from outside, the relationship is likely to be perceived as in- tense, deep, engaged, devoted, insulated and worldly-wise.

Description of the relationship when both parties feel under pressure

When the interaction is restrictive, accusatory, destructive and demoti- vating, the Four will feel incredibly alone, as the Five is a master of with- drawing and physically removing him/herself from the relationship. The objective side of the Five drives the much more emotional Four crazy, while the many feelings and considerable verbosity get on the Five's nerves.

Type 5s are in no way self-absorbed, but they *are* absorbed in that field or hobby that interests them. There will therefore be a lot of talk about topics that are not particularly personal and which the Four is often un- able to relate to. Conversely, the Four is deeply self-absorbed and wish- es that the Five would also be deeply immersed within the Four's inner universe. Typically, the Five will not make a great many demands of the Four, while the Four will make a lot of demands of the Five about how the latter should be there for the Four, and engage with and relate to the Four.

Description of the measures that may bring the partners closer to each other

Each of them is a lone wolf who does not really need others. They are happy to be in their own company without feeling lonely and, indeed, this is almost the Five's preferred state. Both enjoy a rich inner universe, which they want to share with the other in such a way that they can feel safe in the knowledge that the other is able to accommodate them in all their complexity. Type 5 has a Rejection-relationship with both Figures, while Type 4 has a Frustration-relationship with both Figures, so one might say that their relationship with each other is a heated affair, in that both parties are quickly overwhelmed by each other and by the other's requirements about how they should engage with each other within the relationship.

It is recommended that Type 4 works with his/her objectivity and that Type 5 works on his/her ability to relate to the other.

Relationship between Type 4 and Type 6

Description of the relationship when both partners feel resourceful

When the interaction is enriching, supportive, inspiring and evolving, the Four will be supportive and warm, while the Six will be engaging and able to relate to the other. Typically, the Four will be bring the trusting and spontaneous side out of the Six, while the Six will inspire forgiveness and practicality. At the same time, the Four will contribute to the rela- tionship with depth and aesthetic awareness, while the Six will contrib- ute a belief that everything will be all right in the end.

Both Types will contribute to a relationship in which there will be room for emotional and frustrated outbursts without the other becom- ing frightened or withdrawing. They are both focussed on what it is to be human and on the human qualities that each brings to the relationship, and this inner focus within the relationship will generate a robust soli- darity founded upon true appreciation and loyalty.

Viewed from outside, the relationship is likely to be perceived as ex- plosive but stable, human and founded upon strong values around soli- darity and respect.

Description of the relationship when both partners feel under pressure

When the interaction is limiting, accusatory, destructive and demotivat- ing, the Four will feel that they are controlled by the Six's project – that they are merely an object, resource or instrument for the Six. They are both explosive Types who are quick to express their dissatisfaction, but such that the Four is likely to implode and fall apart internally, and the Six is likely to vacillate between externally directed dissatisfaction and internal passive aggression. Type 4s will feel that they are never appreciated – particularly in a relationship with a Six, who has a tendency to vacillate between being welcoming and rejecting. This ambiguity is difficult for the Four to deal with, while the Six will feel that nothing can be relied upon or related to in a concrete way. This relationship is rife with landmines that the other party can easily step on – thereby damaging the relationship on a regular basis.

Description of the measures that may bring the partners closer to each other

Both parties have a temperament such that they believe that by reacting they can get the other to behave in the way they want the other to behave. Type 4 will attempt to manipulate the Six into position, creating a deep insecurity within the Six. Conversely, the Six will use his/her ambiguous approach to test the Four's loyalty. Type 4 has a Frustration-relationship with both Figures, which gives the Six a headache every single day as (s) he tries to guess what it is that must be done correctly to keep the Four happy. Type 6 has an Attachment-relationship with the Protective Figure and therefore seeks something that is stable and sustainable in the Four
– but which is probably the last thing the Four can provide to the Six.

It is recommended that the Type 4 works on understanding his/her manipulative side and that Type 6 works on understanding the "split" aspects of his/her personality.

Relationship between Type 4 and Type 7

Description of the relationship when both partners feel resourceful

When the interaction is enriching, supportive, inspiring and evolving, the Four will be bubbly and nurturing, while the Seven will be attentive and focussed. Typically, the Four will bring the more creative and artistic side out of the Seven, while the Seven will inspire greater audacity. At the same time, the Four will contribute to the relationship with a sense for the aesthetic and life-affirming, while the Seven will contribute lightness and opportunity.

Both Types will contribute to a relationship that is full of life, enjoyable and chaotic in a creative way. This focus on something that is deeper or inner will mutually inspire both parties, and they may often be regarded as the other's muse. They will construct a mutual relationship in which, with a glint in the eye, they are able to build confidence in each other and the desire to act on impulse.

Viewed from outside, the relationship is likely to be perceived as vivacious, magical, lively, enjoyable, boundless and playful.

Description of the relationship when both partners feel under pressure

When the interaction is restrictive, accusatory, destructive and demotivating, the Four will feel disregarded by the Seven's more simplistic mind-set and will sense that the Seven is too keen to find quick solutions for the Four's (problematic) inner universe. The Seven will feel restricted and frustrated by the many emotions that occupy the Four, every minute of every hour of every day, transporting the Four from their experiences of the past to their dealings in the present to their dreams for the future.

Type 4 will have difficulty dealing with Seven's sharp tongue and deprecating approach, while the Seven will often prefer to laugh at the Four's depressive, pessimistic assertions. Both have a tendency to withdraw, such that the Four withdraws into his/her inner universe while also sending out dramatically provocative signals to the Seven, while the Seven simply withdraws mentally, or physically leaves home.

Description of the measures that may bring the partners closer together

Both tend to be full of life, but the Four can seem too deep and the Sev- en can seem too superficial. While it is their liveliness, creativeness and originality that unites them, an internal sense of loss and grief divides them. Type 4 has a Frustration-relationship with both Figures, while the Seven has a Frustration-relationship with the Nurturing Figure. This means that they both very much expect to be able to be vigorous, wor- ry-free and nourished in their relationship and that the other should be active in creating a good spirit within it. The Frustration-relationship also means that they both demand that the one supplies something that there is no chance of the other providing.

It is recommended that Type 4 works on his/her discipline and that Type 7 works on connecting with the Four (and thereby with him/her- self) emotionally.

Relationship between Type 4 and Type 8

Description of the relationship when both partners feel resourceful

When the interaction is enriching, supportive, inspiring and evolving, the Four will be supportive and full of life, while the Eight will be fear- less about the potential of the relationship itself. Typically, the Four will bring the more sensitive and gentle side out of the Eight, while the Eight will inspire action and a will to fight for values, dreams or rights.

Both Types will contribute with vibrancy and initiative, and they will be sharply focussed on the relationship. This internal relationship will be filled with passion, antagonisms and tears. They will devour each other, be there for each other and make use of each other.

Viewed from outside, the relationship is likely to be perceived as excit- ing, lively, explosive, multifaceted, passionate and dynamic.

Description of the relationship when both partners feel under pressure

When the interaction is restrictive, accusatory, destructive and demo- tivating, the Four will feel depressed, under pressure, lost and empty. Conversely, the Eight will feel pressurised by the many demands and emotions, feeling that there is no place for the Eight as (s)he once was.

Type 4 will feel that it is exhausting to be in a relationship with the Eight because of the energy, high tempo and strident disconnect in- volved when the Eight freezes them out. Type 8 will feel that it is exhaust- ing to be always discussing feelings, relationships, solidarity and com- mon values, and that (s)he has to go to great lengths to ensure that the Four does not secure all the power in the relationship.

Description of the measures that may bring the partners closer to each other

Both parties have a marked tendency to berate and criticise the other and to talk openly about how impossible and demanding the other is. There are voids in the relationship that are often filled with strident dis- cussions and arguments. From the Eight's perspective, these can quickly blow over, but a heated discussion remains with the Four for a long time. They both have a great need to be accepted by the other, and, more than in other relationships, these Types need the other party to notice them first, before they notice the other party. Type 4 has a Frustration-rela- tionship with both Figures, which means that the Eight has almost no chance of ever doing anything right for the Four, while the Eight has a Rejection-relationship with the Nurturing Figure and therefore finds it difficult to provide exactly what the Eight basically desires.

It is recommended that Type 4 works on his/her sense of being lost and that Type 8 works on finding common emotional ground with the Four.

Relationship between Type 4 and Type 9

Description of the relationship when both partners feel resourceful

When the interaction is enriching, supportive, inspiring and evolving, the Four will be patient and tolerant, while the Nine will be expressive and creative. Typically, the Four will encourage the livelier and life-af- firming side of the Nine, while the Nine will bring out a more profound and disciplined aspect of the Four. The Four will also contribute to the relationship with spontaneity, pleasure and an aesthetic sense, while the Nine will contribute with calmness, decisiveness and bodily wisdom.

Both Types will contribute to a partnership in which both emerge from their den or their own inner universe and take a realistic position with regard to the world and to the situations they have to face on occa- sion. They both have a tendency to be happy in their own company and to be alone with their thoughts and feelings, and, while the Four has a tendency to feel dissatisfied with his/her inner universe, the Nine tends to romanticise his/her inner universe.

Viewed from outside, the relationship is likely to be perceived as pro- found, calm, respectful, life-affirming and at ease with itself.

Description of the relationship when both partners feel under pressure

When the interaction is restrictive, accusatory, destructive and demoti- vating, the Four will be provoked by the Nine's indecisiveness and (from the Four's perspective) lack of interest. Conversely, the Nine will appear happy and content outwardly, but inwardly harbour feelings of rage, hate and denunciation. This dissonance between the Nine's inner and outer worlds is sensed by the Four, who may begin to pressurise the Nine to say something, share something or express something. This pressure on the Nine simply makes them shut down even more, without, however, leav- ing their physical location (for example, the kitchen or apartment) and they therefore fill a space in the location – without actually occupying it. Type 4 will have a sense that the Nine is not genuinely putting an effort into the relationship and will not acknowledge that there is an issue to discuss; this lack of interest is interpreted by the Four as a lack of interest in the relationship itself. Type 9 will feel under pressure and provoked by the Four's outbursts, accusations and manipulations, and, as probably the most stubborn of all Types, the Nine will attempt to make the situation go away by doing nothing.

Description of the measures that may bring the partners closer to each other

Both parties have a powerful tendency to withdraw into themselves. The Four's inner universe is not always positive and full of life, while the Nine's inner universe is pleasant and comfortable, so it is easier for the Nine to maintain any withdrawal than it is for the Four. While the Nine hopes that the hard times disappear by themselves, the Four will chal- lenge, provoke and incite confrontation. Type 4 has a Frustration-re- lationship with both the Nurturing and the Protective Figures, which means that the Four can always find fault with the Nine and is more eas- ily frustrated with the Nine – and with the relationship as a whole. Type 9 has an Attachment (or ambivalent)-relationship with both the Protec- tive and Nurturing Figures, meaning that the Nine cannot truly perceive him/herself in the relationship and is therefore easily overwhelmed by constantly having to take a position with regard to the relationship – as is often necessary in a relationship with a Type 4.

It is recommended that Type 4 works on owning his/her own feelings of frustration and not showering the Nine with them instead, and that the Nine works on creating harmony between his/her inner and outer worlds.

Relationship between Type 5 and Type 5

Description of the relationship when both partners feel resourceful

When the interaction is enriching, supportive, inspiring and evolving, the two Fives will relate to each other and cultivate honesty. They will contribute to a relationship in which they bring out the other's person- ality in a level-headed but loving way, and they will empathically and truthfully encourage each other to perceive themselves with sincerity and love.

They will both contribute to a relationship in which the truth about what it is to be human – and to be that person one actually is – is fun- damental to the relationship and, like two druids, they will make use of completely new psychological, spiritual, naturalistic, emotional and so- matic methods to unveil the truth in each other.

Viewed from outside, the relationship is likely to be perceived as wise, real, true, playful, teasing, mysterious, experimental and spiritual in a practical way.

Description of the relationship when both partners feel under pressure

When the interaction is restrictive, accusatory, destructive and demoti- vating, both Fives will shut the other out and function quite effectively without the presence and interference of the other. They will constant- ly encounter their own dark side because the other is so clearly stupid, emotional, closed down, useless, valueless, lost, inconsistent and se- duced by the wrong norms and attitudes. They will instil in the other the feeling of being brainless, useless and worthless, which is precisely what the Five fears in him/herself.

Description of the measures that may bring the partners closer to each other

Both Fives perceive themselves to be supremely gifted and enjoy being together with someone who is also gifted. However, there is a tendency for the first gifted partner to shower the second gifted partner with their "gifts". When one of the Fives propounds their theory as to why, for ex- ample, the relationship has problems, the other will deliver their own ex- planatory commentary, which in reality simply rejects what the first has said. They both have a Rejection-relationship with both Figures, mean- ing that, for most of their lives, Fives have had to learn about the qualities represented by both Figures. Neither Five-partner has really learned to relate to the other, show empathy, set norms in life or reach compro- mises within a family or close relationship. They therefore flounder in their demands of each other, which they can neither live up to nor pro- vide themselves. However, when the Five-couple do manage to evolve together, they will have worked through critical elements of their habits and patterns (often traumatic) in connection with their Object Relation. That is to say, in practice, that the Fives evolve the attributes represented by both Figures, which is fundamentally about navigating a society that is built upon cooperation, interaction and cohesion.

It is recommended that they work on developing empathy – specif- ically the capacity to convey curiosity about the emotional universe of others, and on investigating precisely how their Object Relation can be that place where they achieve the great breakthrough in their personal development.

Relationship between Type 5 and Type 6

Description of the relationship when both partners feel resourceful

When the interaction is enriching, supportive, inspiring and evolving, the Five will be lively and loyal, while the Six will be patient and able to relate. Typically, the Five will bring the calmer side out of the Six, while the Six will inspire action and leadership. The Five will also contribute to the relationship by exploring the more essential aspects of life (and thereby also the relationship itself), while the Six will contribute a capac- ity for action and process.

Both Types will ensure that the relationship is genuine, loyal and warm – this warmth deriving primarily from their humour, the Five's ra- zor-sharp and the Six's more whimsical. On the one hand they do not have a particularly sharp mutual focus on the relationship itself, in that they respect each other as being of equal worth, but on the other hand they tend to stand together when it really counts.

Viewed from outside, the relationship is likely to be perceived as sta- ble, calm, quiet, subtle, warm, unproblematic and loyal.

Description of the relationship when both partners feel under pressure

When the interaction is restrictive, accusatory, destructive and demo- tivating, the Five will withdraw and roll out their profoundly objective, unfeeling and rejecting attitude, which will provoke the Six, who needs a partner to engage with them emotionally. Type 6 will attempt to push the Five in order to get a reaction or sentiment out of them – which simply leads to the Five beginning to withdraw and to feel violated by the Six.

Type 5 will have a tendency to feel violated and disrespected by the

Six, and will begin to explain why the Six is mistaken and why the Five is right. Conversely, the Six will believe that mind-reading is possible and expect notable reactions from the Five (which never manifest them- selves) and will therefore begin to feel that they are the adult in the re- lationship – a view that is reinforced by the Five's tendency to smoulder passively…so passively that their disenchantment makes itself obvious. When the Five begins to withdraw, the Six can get a feeling of betrayal and therefore lose faith in the Five's loyalty.

Description of the measures that may bring the partners closer to each other

Both have a rational orientation toward the relationship, although the Five is the more rational and emotionally closed of the two. Type 6 is not always rational and is prone to emotional, irrational outbursts, whose il- logical explosiveness confuses the Five. Type 5 has a Rejection-relation- ship with both Figures, meaning that the Five demands to be noticed, heard and accommodated by the Six, while the Six must also be con- sistent in his/her attitudes and opinions. Type 6 has an Attachment-re- lationship with the Protective Figure, which means that the Six needs to be able to rely on the Five and therefore demands extraordinary levels of loyalty and stability.

It is recommended that Type 5 works on the way in which he/she shuts out the other within the relationship and that Type 6 works on his/ her lack of clarity in word and deed.

Relationship between Type 5 and Type 7

Description of the relationship when both partners feel resourceful

When the interaction is enriching, supportive, inspiring and evolving, the Five will be full of ideas and able to relate, while the Seven will be practical and dedicated. Typically, the Five will bring out the more profound, thoughtful and focussed side of the Seven, while the Seven will inspire a capacity to bring good ideas into play. The Five will also contribute to the relationship having weight and substance, while the Seven will contribute with liveliness and practicality. Both Types will contribute to a relationship that has a love of learning, can think outside the box, and has focus and originality. They do not necessarily focus on each other or the relationship itself, and they can easily function alone without the other. Where the Five can easily shut down within the relationship and simply be in their own company, the Seven will disappear from the relationship and seek out other, livelier places with more energy. One the one hand, this focus on something else will build an effortless relationship, while on the other the relationship may become fragile in the face of significant challenges.

Viewed from outside, the relationship is likely to be perceived as inventive, thoughtful, intellectual, dedicated and focussed on projects or tasks that typically will have nothing to do with the relationship.

Description of the relationship when both partners feel under pressure

When the interaction is restrictive, accusatory, destructive and demotivating, the Five will withdraw and will not beat around the bush in articulating his/her views on the Seven's ways. This cold and emotionally blank behaviour will frustrate the Seven so that they will give up, escape or turn their back on the Five. Conversely, the Seven will be derogatory, critical and sarcastic, which is regarded by the Five as infantile, foolish and stupid. In this relationship it is easy for the one to ignore the oth- er, to actually physically leave the other, and simply not give the other a passing thought. They will not, however, regard a separation as a break- up of the relationship, but simply as a means to avoid being emotional together.

Type 5 would like the Seven to understand the way things are connect- ed and will fight for the relationship as long as they feel that the Seven is listening and taking on board the things the Five has to say. Type 7 would like the Five to make things simpler, easily accessible and not as abstract – but does not explain this to the Five.

Description of the measures that may bring the partners closer to each other

Both are good at leaving the other alone and almost not bothering about the other – in a positive way. This is understood to mean that they do not necessarily say so many foolish things to the other that there is no way back. Neither of them is particularly interested in being involved when emotional sparks are flying, so in the short run it can be sensible simply to extricate themselves from the discussion and let things lie. Type 5s have a Rejection-relationship with both Figures, which means that they would be happy for the Seven to provide the necessary care, trust and support, while the Seven should also supply wisdom and stability. But this feels restrictive to the Seven, who absolutely does not want this re- sponsibility for the relationship. Type 7s have a Frustration-relationship with the Nurturing Figure, meaning that they want the Five to provide the space for their vulnerability and their need for engagement to be ac- commodated, which is not always something at which the Five excels.

It is recommended that Type 5 works on relating to the Seven and that Type 7 works on giving time and space to the Five.

Relationship between Type 5 and Type 8

Description of the relationship when both partners feel resourceful

When the interaction is enriching, supportive, inspiring and evolving, the Five will be clear-headed and expressive, while the Eight will love learning and be able to relate. Typically, the Five will bring out the more profound, wise and truth-seeking side of the Eight, while the Eight will inspire vigour, courage and sincerity. The Five will also contribute to the relationship with vulnerability, innocence and curiosity, while the Eight will contribute with clear frameworks and by sensitively challenging Five's assertions and ideas.

Both Types will contribute to a relationship in which vulnerability and humility are possible and their common focus will be on truths, the authentic, the real and the genuine. Their shared focus is not necessarily on the relationship itself; when it *is* the focus, both partners will exhibit an unconditional loyalty.

Viewed from outside, the relationship is likely to be perceived as worldly-wise, dedicated, vigorous, courageous, humble and focussed.

Description of the relationship when both partners feel under pressure

When the interaction is restrictive, accusatory, destructive and demotivating, the Five will feel violated...to the point of feeling intimidated and overwhelmed. It is apparent that the Five thinks that the Eight is stupid, childish and a cheap instrument whose only function is to cause dam- age. Conversely, the Eight will feel provoked by the Five, who the Eight finds arrogant, inconsistent and a "know-it-all".

Type 5 will see the relationship as an institution and have many clear opinions about what such an institution ought to express, contain and manage, while Type 8 will see the relationship as a framework for loyalty and will demand that the partners devote themselves, sacrifice them- selves and express themselves (so that they both know where they stand with each other). Type 5 will instil a sense of stupidity in the Eight, while the Eight will instil a feeling of powerlessness and insignificance in the Five.

Description of the measures that may bring the partners closer to each other

Both parties are deeply anxious about being spurned or dumped, and they both have a strategic sense that it is better to do the dumping than to be dumped. Thus, both are quick to end the relationship with the view that this is justifiable and that the other party is fundamentally to blame for the break-up. There is not necessarily any disappointment attached to the fact of the other not behaving as expected, but rather a loss of feel- ing, an arrogant and unemotional closure. Type 5s have a Rejection-rela- tionship with both Figures, meaning that they will demand that the Eight supplies the qualities of both the Nurturing and the Protective Figures. Type 8s have a Rejection-relationship with the Nurturing Figure and demand that the Five supplies care, latitude and understanding for the Eight.

It is recommended that Type 5 works on expressing him/herself clear- ly and unambiguously (and chooses his/her battles carefully), and that Type 8 works on awakening his/her curiosity and desire to learn.

Relationship between Type 5 and Type 9

Description of the relationship when both partners feel resourceful

When the interaction is enriching, supportive, inspiring and evolving, the Five will be clear and able to relate, while the Nine will be expressive and strong-willed. Typically, the Five will bring out the livelier and more dedicated side of the Nine, while the Nine will inspire gentleness and help bring the Five's knowledge to life. The Five will also contribute to a relationship with vulnerability and humility, while the Nine will contrib- ute with a warmth that makes the relationship less sombre.

Both Types will contribute with calm, balance, contact with their "inner universe" (without this becoming emotional) and will focus on truths and that which makes a difference. They do not necessarily fo- cus on the relationship itself, but rather on their individual universe and that of their partner. Over time, they are able to build a close partnership based upon a deep, mutual respect for each other.

Viewed from outside, the relationship is likely to be perceived as gen- tle, stable, calm, balanced, wise, warm and humble.

Description of the relationship when both partners feel under pressure

When the interaction is restrictive, accusatory, destructive and demoti- vating, the Five will feel provoked by the Nine's stubbornness or passive aggression. They will regard the Nine as stupid and out of control, and they will, through their objective and unfeeling form of communication, end up hurting the Nine personally. Conversely, the Nine will feel pro- voked by the Five's ability to destroy the Nine's fabulous, or picture-post- card, conceptions of the relationship, friendships, love or eternal life.

While Five has the capacity to frighten others with substantiated facts about the extermination of life, this will often shatter Nine's fantastic dream-like imaginings about life.

Typically, the Five will quickly shut the Nine out, which actually suits the Nine fine – except that this is also the Nine's approach, although in a less consistent way. The Nine's reaction is also to shut down, which the Five can comfortably live with, simply increasing his/her level of arrogance and coldness.

Description of the measures that may bring the partners closer to each other

Both partners find it easy to live in their own inner world, although the Five's inner world is bleaker, scarier and creepier than the Nine's. They are not necessarily lonely when they are alone, and their calm tempera- ment can be to their common advantage in many ways, in that they can both feel a connection without having to be in close contact the whole time. Type 5 has a Rejection-relationship with both Figures, while Type 9 has an Attachment-relationship with both Figures. This means that they both have difficulties demonstrating the qualities of both Figures them- selves and partly expect the other to demonstrate them. At the same time, there is a certain tolerance about the fact that it is fundamentally difficult to live up to or demonstrate the qualities represented by the Figures.

It is recommended that Type 5 works on relating to the Nine and that Type 9 works on making him/herself clear to the Five.

Relationship between Type 6 and Type 6

Description of the relationship when both partners feel resourceful

When the interaction is enriching, supportive, inspiring and evolving, the two Sixes will offer guidance and invite the personal leadership of the other. They will contribute to a relationship in which they help each other to find the courage to follow their heart as well as to develop a cer- tain bodily empathy, such that they listen to themselves and trust their intuition.

They will both contribute to a relationship in which uncertainty is a strength, allowing both of them to move forward with an open mind; this will also assist in illuminating whatever needs to be illuminated. They will both discover their own form of leadership in the world, which does not necessarily include the other. For example, one of the Sixes could become the national leader of the scout movement while other becomes the chief programmer for a security firm.

Viewed from the outside, the relationship is likely to be perceived as loyal, independent, supportive, dedicated, guiding, principled, united and practical.

Description of the relationship when both partners feel under pressure

When the interaction is restrictive, accusatory, destructive and demotivat- ing, both Sixes will experience extreme reactions toward the other, who obviously takes decisions on behalf of the relationship that have not been thought through or included all perspectives. Both Sixes will believe that mind-reading exists and that the other ought to be able to understand what the first Six is thinking and has experienced. They will constantly en-

counter their own dark side, given that the other will be dependent, irresponsible, will act without thought, be emotional, obstinate, a lone wolf, and someone who has not mastered the skills that they have. They will in- stil in the other the feeling of being irresponsible and someone who does not think things through and who lacks skills and projects of his/her own
– which are precisely those things that the Six fears in him/herself.

Description of the measures that may bring the partners closer to each other

Both Sixes take great pride in the undertakings they take on and will do whatever they can to ensure that their tasks or assignments are carried out with the greatest possible insight and responsibility. They are team players and often become spokespeople for causes that include others (for example, the scout movement, homosexual rights, the organisation of underpaid workers at a burger chain). The Six wants (requires) the other Six to support them in their mission and to sacrifice themselves to the same extent that the first Six does. It is, of course, impossible for both to sacrifice themselves or support the other 100 percent, a fact that often leads to heated debates and feelings of disappointment, frustration and impotence. They both have an Attachment-relationship with the Protec- tive Figure, which means they have a rather diffuse attitude toward what their direction in life really is and, when they finally discover what is im- portant for them, they will give all they have for the cause...and want the other to follow them. However, when the Six-couple succeed in evolving together, they will have worked through critical elements of their habits and patterns (often traumatic) in connection with their Object Relation. That is to say, in practice, that the Six will take up their personal leader- ship with their heart set on the right course and with a perseverance and self-discipline that inspires others around them.

It is recommended that they work on establishing contact with their longings and ambitions as well as developing the courage to live out their calling, such that their Object Relation can be precisely that place where they achieve the great breakthrough in their personal development.

Relationship between Type 6 and Type 7

Description of the relationship when both partners feel resourceful

When the interaction is enriching, supportive, inspiring and evolving, the Six will be well-balanced and vigorous, while the Seven will be grate- ful and full of energy. Typically, the Six will bring out a more appreciative side of the Seven – particularly with regard to family and friends, while the Seven will inspire play and hedonism.

Both Types will contribute with appreciation and recognition – particularly for any children within the relationship – and this appreciation and recognition will get all the partners to grow and build up a powerful sense of self-esteem and self-acceptance.

Viewed from outside, the relationship is likely to be perceived as stable, lively, experimental, well-balanced and loyal.

Description of the relationship when both partners feel under pressure

When the interaction is restrictive, accusatory, destructive and demotivating, the Six will withdraw and leave the stage to the Seven, while criticising the Seven behind closed doors. The Type 7 has an even great- er capacity to criticise; however, this does not take place behind closed doors, but directly and publicly – and, as such, this is a more destructive tendency than the Six's.

Type 6s will feel that it is they who expend all the effort on the relationship and that the Seven just fritters it all away, while the Seven feels that even the relationship itself is a restriction that just takes an all-too-narrow view of the concepts of "relationship" and "loyalty to one's partner". They each fight their own fight within the relationship, with the Six focussing on solidarity, while the Seven attempts to create happiness within and for the relationship.

Description of the measures that may bring the partners closer to each other

Both fight within and for the relationship, with an orientation toward loyalty leading the Six to try to unite the relationship, while an orienta- tion toward opportunity leads the Seven to try to make it possible to be in a steady relationship that is dynamic, free and rewarding. Type 6 takes a great deal for granted (a faith in mind-reading), while the Seven would rather be free to take something for granted. Their abilities to provoke and challenge are equally well developed, but their conversations rarely reach their conclusion with a solution. Type 6 has an Attachment-rela- tionship with the Protective Figure, while the Seven has a Frustration-re- lationship with the Nurturing Figure. This means that the Six expects a higher level of stability from the Seven than it is in the latter's nature to provide, and the Seven expects to be accommodated and endured in all their ways of being.

It is recommended that Type 6 works on dropping his/her faith in mind-reading and that Type 7 works on expressing his/her expectations and their consequences clearly.

Relationship between Type 6 and Type 8

Description of the relationship when both parties feel resourceful

When the interaction is enriching, supportive, inspiring and evolving, the Six will be encouraging and balancing, while the Eight will be sup- portive and able to relate. Typically, Type 6 will bring out the more loyal and team-oriented (family-oriented) side of the Eight, while the Eight will inspire leadership and a down-to-earth approach. The Six will also contribute to a relationship with focus on solidarity and interaction, while the Eight will contribute with sympathetic personal leadership.

Both Types will contribute to the relationship with solidarity: they "have each other's back". There will be an inner focus on the relation- ship as something valuable, a place where a foundation can be built for a shared future. If there are children in the relationship, there will be a sharp focus on creating a solid foundation and good opportunities for the children.

Viewed from outside, the relationship is likely to be perceived as dedi- cated, energetic, loyal, faithful, supportive, unified and respectful.

Description of the relationship when both partners feel under pressure

When the interaction is restrictive, accusatory, destructive and demo- tivating, the Six will feel that the Eight always wants the last word, that the Eight expresses opinions about which they have no knowledge, and that the Eight has a tendency to be more loyal to other relationships. This creates insecurity for the Six, who begins to question the loyalty of the Eight. Conversely, the Eight will become insecure about the Six because of the latter's natural lack of trust and need to put the Eight's loyalty and wisdom to the test. This mutual testing of the relationship often results in energetic discussions in which each partner demands that the other tangibly demonstrate their faith in, or loyalty to, the relationship.

Type 6 will feel that (s)he is, by definition, the more loyal of the partners, while the Eight has the same perception of *him/her*self. Type 6 worries about the relationship and therefore undertakes lots of projects to keep the relationship together or to ensure its wellbeing. Type 8 assumes considerable responsibility within the relationship and therefore works hard, in his/her own way, to do what is best for it. Typically, neither partner realises quite how hard or seriously the other works on behalf of the relationship.

Description of the measures that may bring the partners closer to each other

Both partners have an energetic temperament, but the Six is more searching and probing toward the Eight, while the Eight is more direct and provocative. Both partners provoke each other, in fact, but each in their own way, such that the Six does not recognise their own behaviour as provocative, while the Eight is quite clear that they provoke in order to test the Six's limits. Type 6 has an Attachment-relationship with the Protective Figure, meaning that they expect the Eight to demonstrate an unambiguous loyalty, trust and support. However, because the Eight is also loyal to, for example, childhood friends, colleagues and clients, the Six has a sense that they are not fully supported. Type 8 has a Re- jection-relationship with the Nurturing Figure, meaning that they also demand the Six's loyalty, to the extent that this reflects the qualities rep- resented by the Nurturing Figure. This means that the Eight expects that, no matter how they may behave, the Six will continue to care about them (in the same way as a mother will typically put up with her child's clumsy antics).

It is recommended that Type 6 works on his/her ambiguous challeng- ing of the Eight and that Type 8 works on his/her harsh and occasionally brutal tone toward the Six.

Relationship between Type 6 and Type 9

Description of the relationship when both partners feel resourceful

When the interaction is enriching, supportive, inspiring and evolving, the Six will be vibrant and cheerful, while the Nine will be dedicated and back the other up. Typically, the Six will bring out the more dedicated and ex- pressive side of the Nine, while the Nine will inspire sensitive leadership in the Six. The Six will also contribute to the relationship with latitude and optimism, while the Nine will contribute with accessibility and latitude.

Both Types will contribute to the relationship with calmness and sta- bility, and by challenging each other to bring the best out of each indi- vidual. They will have a more personal focus within the relationship than on the relationship itself, thereby building over time a relationship that has more of the character of a deep, lifelong friendship.

Viewed from outside, the relationship is likely to be perceived as car- ing, dedicated, supportive, conciliatory, deep and mutually respectful.

Description of the relationship when both parties feel under pressure

When the interaction is restrictive, accusatory, destructive and demo- tivating, the Six will challenge and test the Nine's limits, which is prob- ably the last thing the Nine can cope with in this relationship. The Six's vacillation between everything being fine and everything being awful is difficult to deal with for the Nine, who simply reacts with defiance (pas- sive aggression) or by shutting down and being present in body but not in spirit. Conversely, the Nine's ability not to take decisions, not to take a position and not to stand up for his/her beliefs is a challenge for the Six, as these are precisely what the Six demands from a relationship.

Type 6 will feel that it is they who fight for the relationship while the Nine just seems to be along for the ride. Type 9 also feels that they fight for the relationship, but they do so by making themselves less visible and thereby not being the cause of problems. Both are naturally of the opin- ion that they work hard to keep things together, but neither of them understand, or have any need for, the way the other does this.

Description of the measures that may bring the partners closer to each other

Both partners have a marked tendency to believe that mind-reading is possible. This means that they are both convinced that they do things for the right reason and that the other ought to understand the background and back them up in their actions. Type 6 has an Attraction-relationship with the Protective Figure and therefore has an expectation that the Nine speaks unambiguously, stands by his/her opinions and expresses these in such a way that the Six can orient him/herself accordingly. Type 9, likewise, has an Attraction-relationship, but to both Figures, and there- fore has great expectations that the Six will supply all the qualities of both Figures – and as a minimum does not make demands of the Nine with regard to qualities originating from either Figure.

It is recommended that Type 6 works on his/her desire to challenge the Nine and that Type 9 works on being clear and letting the Six know when (s)he starts his/her guessing game for which there is no correct answer.

Relationship between Type 7 and Type 7

Description of the relationship when both partners feel resourceful

When the interaction is enriching, supportive, inspiring and evolving, the two Sevens will be attentive, focussed and lively with each other. They will contribute to a relationship in which there is a place for both play and profundity, and each will be the other's best "playmate".

They will both contribute to a relationship in which there are opportunities to explore life, start up initiatives "just because it could be exciting", enjoy what should be enjoyed and experience what should be experienced. They will be soulmates and create a relationship that can push the boundaries of what can be experienced and enjoyed.

Viewed from outside, the relationship is likely to be perceived as live- ly, adventurous, innovative, boundless, experimental, enjoyable, rich in experiences, energetic and entertaining.

Description of the relationship when both parties feel under pressure

When the interaction is restrictive, accusatory, destructive and demotivating, both Sevens will be frustrated that the other is too boring, unengaged and rigid. Both will be critical and sarcastic in their frontal attacks on the other, and they will have fun at the other's expense. They will constantly encounter their own dark side, because the other will be sluggish, petulant, boring, listless, disengaged, obdurate, inflexible, frugal, passive and lifeless. They will instil in the other a feeling of being rigid, inhibited and trapped, which is precisely what the Seven fears in him/herself.

Description of the measures that may bring the partners closer to each other

Both Sevens need to test boundaries and to be experimental, while also needing the other to be capable of being serious, profound and attentive with them. Both Sevens often lose contact with their own feelings or in- ner universe, but want the other to be sufficiently attentive to create fo- cus and "presence". However, because both of them distract themselves and are therefore not really attentive themselves, they will become frus- trated over the other and begin to blame the other for the lack of close- ness within the relationship. They both have a Frustration-relationship with the Nurturing Figure and therefore demand that the other supplies precisely those qualities the Nurturing Figure represents.

However, when the Seven-couple succeed in evolving together, they will have worked through critical elements of their habits and patterns (often traumatic) in connection with their Object Relation. That is to say, in practice, that the Seven will discover their inner universe and accept their self-discoveries, which will require great focus, presence and atten- tiveness.

It is recommended that they work on developing empathy for them- selves, attentiveness and a deep relationship with their need to be no- ticed, heard and fully accommodated, such that their Object Relation is precisely the place where they can achieve the great breakthrough in their personal development.

Relationship between Type 7 and Type 8

Description of the relationship when both partners feel resourceful

When the interaction is enriching, supportive, inspiring and evolving, the Seven will be precise and embracing, while the Eight will be gen- tle and supportive. Typically, the Seven will bring out the more caring and joyful side of the Eight, while the Eight will inspire an ability to join in, and back out of, the right things. Both partners will contribute to an active relationship, in which there is focus on what has meaning in life. They will have firm principles or values to manage and guide the rela- tionship, and although they will enjoy many activities as individuals, they will also construct a common framework together – particularly if there are children in the relationship.

Viewed from outside, the relationship is likely to be perceived as en- terprising, sparkling, genuine/honest, nurturing, active and gentle.

Description of the relationship when both partners feel under pressure

When the interaction is restrictive, accusatory, destructive and demoti- vating, the Seven will feel overwhelmed by the Eight, who has the idea that their Seven partner can handle all their bodily and energy outbursts. Conversely, the Eight will feel limited by the Seven's vague proposals, suggestions, ideas, concepts and principles. The Seven's flightiness will create a sense of frustration, impotence and anger in the Eight.

Type 7 will feel that it is they who are the flexible, solution-oriented and pliable partner, and therefore have the right to be granted some ac- knowledgement when they have experimented with things. Type 8 will feel that they are the one who works hard, pulls out all the stops and has all the responsibility on their shoulders (particularly because they can- not rely on the Seven) – and has therefore earned the right to do as they wish.

Description of the measures that may bring the partners closer to each other

As described, both types have the feeling that they offer something to the relationship and therefore have earned the right to enjoy the free- doms that might be valuable to them as individuals. Type 7 has a Frus- tration-relationship with the Nurturing Figure, while Type 8 has a Rejec- tion-relationship. This results in both parties believing that the other will put up with anything whatsoever (just as the Nurturing Figure will put up with whatever the baby does), while they themselves are unable to demonstrate this unconditional love to themselves.

It is recommended that Type 7 works on setting boundaries and being less flexible, and that Type 8 works on recognising their partner as the person who tolerates all their outbursts.

Relationship between Type 7 and Type 9

Description of the relationship when both partners feel resourceful

When the interaction is enriching, supportive, inspiring and evolving, the Seven will be deep and healing, while the Nine will be lively and will encourage the other. Typically, the Seven will bring the more out- going and communicative side out of the Nine, while the Nine will in- spire deeper and essential discussions. At the same time, the Seven will contribute hedonism and energy to the relationship, while the Nine will contribute with a foundation for quiet and intimate moments.

Both Types will contribute with a positive, future-oriented focus, which is not necessarily directed so much on the relationship itself as on enjoying the now, and toying with notions about the excitements that might occur in the future. This forward-looking outlook encourages the Nine to have an aspiration for the future and the Seven to be more realis- tic about what the future could hold for the relationship.

Viewed from outside, the relationship is likely to be perceived as opti- mistic, able to relate, grateful, energetic and playful.

Description of the relationship when both partners feel under pressure

When the interaction is restrictive, accusatory, destructive and demoti- vating, the Seven will be cutting and sarcastic and will provoke the Nine, who pays the Seven back by not responding. The Seven's high levels of energy can catch the Nine off their guard, leaving the Nine feeling vio- lated and spoken down to. Conversely, the Nine will be obdurate and maintain things the way they are, which frustrates the Seven enormous- ly and who responds by shaking up the established structure with new possibilities. Sevens will tend to start new things up or set things in motion without asking the Nine, just to confirm to themselves that the Nine must not limit them in their chosen way of living.

Type 7 will feel that the Nine is stupid, indolent and disengaged and therefore feels fully justified in initiating things or, indeed, cancelling them without referring to the Nine. Conversely, the Nine will feel that the Seven is childish, insensitive and naïve, and will feel entitled not to engage with someone so infantile. Type 9 possesses a stubbornness that will overcome the Seven's impulse to initiate things – and, in this rela- tionship, it will be stubbornness that wins.

Description of the measures that may bring the partners closer to each other

Both partners want the good life or to experience the positive in the relationship. While the Seven seeks the good life through experiences, the Nine seeks it through stability and steadfastness. In this sense, they are each other's opposites, and what binds them together is a hope that everything will be all right in the end. Type 7 has a Frustration-relation- ship with the Nurturing Figure and therefore expects that the Nine will be able to cope with all their verbal assaults, while the Nine must also be there during exactly those Earth-shattering moments when the Seven comes into contact with their feelings and inner universe. Type 9s have an Attraction-relationship to both Figures, which means that they expect the Seven to compensate for the qualities in both Figures, although, at the same time, the Seven must not be too demanding themselves.

It is recommended that Type 7 works on his/her energy and inconsistency toward the Nine, and that the Nine works on his/her passivity and stubbornness toward the Seven.

Relationship between Type 8 and Type 8

Description of the relationship when both partners feel resourceful

When the interaction is enriching, supportive, inspiring and evolving, the two Eights will be empathic and strong for each other. They will both contribute to a relationship in which there is a place for energy, passion, dedication and the emergence of strength. They will be two giants who support each other and stand shoulder-to-shoulder against a world that can be harsh and unjust.

They will both contribute to a relationship governed by unconditional loyalty, in which they build each other up, pave the way for the other, and build empires from nothing. Their shared creative power will, in all likelihood, be translated into causes, projects or companies which they set up, build and run together.

Viewed from outside, the relationship is likely to be perceived as robust, powerful, dedicated, passionate, courageous, hard-working, energetic and expressive.

Description of the relationship when both partners feel under pressure

When the interaction is restrictive, accusatory, destructive and demotivating, both Eights will be full of anger and madness directed toward the other, with the one feeling that the other threatens their place in the hierarchy. Their war will absorb most of their energy, given that both Eights feel threatened by the other during their every waking moment. They will constantly encounter their own dark side, because the other will be deceptive, manipulative, weak, vulnerable, sensitive, emotional and insane. They will instil in the other the feeling that they lack influence or positivity, that they are weak, insignificant and controlled – which is precisely what the Eight fears in him/herself.

Description of the measures that may bring the partners closer to each other

Both Eights have a deep faith in fair play and loyalty and react strongly if the other shows signs of deceit or manipulation. However, they are both extremely deceitful and manipulative themselves and, as a rule, keep their cards close to their chest, right up to the point that they receive complete and unconditional trust. The challenge, though, is that they are both rejection Types and would rather reject before they are reject- ed, meaning that complete and utter trust comes with tough conditions attached. They both have a Rejection-relationship with the Nurturing Figure and therefore demand to be noticed, heard, listened to, accom- modated and fully embraced by the other, even as they themselves find it difficult to embrace the other so completely and unconditionally. They both have a need to find out about themselves by provoking the other, and as a rule this will take the form of serial provocations, where neither really knows how the whole situation arose.

However, when the Eight-couple do succeed in evolving together, they will have worked through critical elements of their habits and patterns (often traumatic) in connection with their Object Relation. That is to say, in practice, that the Eight will discover that it is not necessary to put pres- sure on the other all the time to check whether the other is still there for them and whether the other can deal with the Eight as the Eight really is. It is recommended that they work on developing trust, curiosity and empathy, without first requiring the other to show trust, curiosity and empathy; they should also work out where precisely their Object Rela- tion can be the place where they can achieve the great breakthrough in their personal development.

Relationship between Type 8 and Type 9

Description of the relationship when both partners feel resourceful

When the interaction is enriching, supportive, inspiring and evolving, the Eight will be the rock against which the Nine can lean, while the Nine will "soften" the Eight. Typically, the Eight will bring the more expressive side out of the Nine, while the Nine will inspire latitude and compassion. The Eight will also contribute to the relationship with humility and ten- derness, while the Nine will contribute with direct dialogue.

Both Types will contribute with solidity and a grounded approach, and they will be sharply focussed on the relationship. This focus on the relationship is an expression of a deep respect and dedicated loyalty, such that it may appear that everything else is not really important. This relationship can appear like two wise old she-elephants who know ex- actly where to go to find life-giving waterholes, that things take time, and that it is all right to make mistakes along the way.

Viewed from outside, the relationship is likely to be perceived as close-knit, robust, uncomplicated, loyal and stubborn.

Description of the relationship when both partners feel under pressure

When the interaction is restrictive, accusatory, destructive and demo- tivating, the Eight will feel powerless in the face of the Nine's passivity and lack of enthusiasm and dedication. This will spark the provocative aspect of the Eight into life, and they will attempt to push the Nine in the hope of generating a reaction. But the reaction never comes, because the Nine will feel violated and forced into taking a position on something about which they are unable to take a position. The Nine therefore stops reacting altogether and, as the Nine also believes in the phenomenon of mind-reading, they will be amazed that the Eight cannot understand, all by him/herself, that provocation does not help.

Type 8 will take on the responsibility for many of the relationship's tasks, activities and projects, and gradually begins to take on the Nine's responsibilities and dedication as well – and later complains that the Nine never accepts his/her responsibilities. Type Nine will happily leave the responsibility for practical matters to the Eight, but fears that there will be a price to pay for not having taken responsibility…and that this price will have to be paid to the Eight at some point.

Description of the measures that may bring the partners closer to each other

Both partners have a strong sense of integrity, meaning that if their gut instinct tells them that something must be done – and particularly if it must *not* be done – it would be almost an act of self-harm to go against this gut instinct. This experience or acting out of integrity alternately re- sembles stubbornness and obduracy, with which both partners in the relationship often meet the other. Type 8s have a Rejection-relationship with the Nurturing Figure, which means that they demand that the Nine accommodates them and all their energy, intensity and their direct ap- proach to things. Type 9s have an Attraction-relationship with both Fig- ures which is so overwhelming that it is easier to disappear into them- selves and their inner universe than to make demands of the world or to allow the world to make demands of them.

It is recommended that Type 8 works on his/her impulse to push the Nine and that the Nine works on setting clear boundaries for the Eight.

Relationship between Type 9 and Type 9

Description of the relationship when both partners feel resourceful

When the interaction is enriching, supportive, inspiring and evolving, the two Nines will be precise, well-meaning, accommodating and firm. They will both contribute to a relationship in which the two back each other up, express their opinions, values and attitudes clearly and unam- biguously, stand by their principles (not only in adversity or when there are things they will not do) and will try to poke the other's stubbornness with humour.

They will both contribute to a relationship in which the internal com- pass is a bodily sense and thereby a physical strength that guides both of them. They will help each other by following their internal compass to get closer to that which may be important for each one of them.

Viewed from outside, the relationship is likely to be perceived as ac- commodating, stable, harmonious, learning, tender, playful and evolving.

Description of the relationship when both partners feel under pressure

When the interaction is restrictive, accusatory, destructive and demoti- vating, both Nines will withdraw into their own inner universe and, by means of a passive-aggressive non-presence, will paralyse the relation- ship, leaving two people in a living room, each with a half-empty cup of cold coffee, staring at different corners of the room. Alternatively, one of them will complain about everything that is not working and that should be different, which the other will respond to by being passively demon- strative. They will constantly encounter their own dark sides because the other will be self-absorbed, will draw attention to him/herself, will overwhelm, will occupy the space in their shared living room, control, dominate and pressurise the other to do things they do not want to do. They will instil in the other the feeling that they are the one causing the splits and conflict – which is precisely what the Nine fears in him/herself.

Description of the measures that may bring the partners closer to each other

Both Nines believe deeply in giving the other space, allowing the other to thrive in their own best way. But this latitude can mean that they are not present themselves and simply allow the other to get on with experi- encing life. If both withdraw (with that best of intentions, namely to give the other space), it will be difficult to them to pay attention to each other within the relationship. They can both demonstrate a degree of latitude toward the other that can, taken to extremes, resemble a lack of interest and which over time can mean that they do not evolve together, mirror themselves in each other, accommodate each other as people in a close relationship, and where they are both just comfortable in each other's company. They both have an Attachment-relationship with both Fig- ures, which means that they have a diffuse or ambivalent way of noticing and accommodating each other within the relationship. This can lead to a type of misunderstood latitude and thereby result in a relationship in which neither notices the other apart from as mere installations or ob- jects in each other's lives. However, when the Nine-couple do succeed in evolving together, they will have worked through critical elements of their habits and patterns (often traumatic) in connection with their Ob- ject Relation. That is to say, in practice, that the Nine will work out that they need to assert themselves and make their voice heard (both to make their viewpoint clear and as a means to speak for themselves) in order to avoid conflicts and imbalances.

It is recommended that they work on developing an unambiguous clarity and, even more, to express what they do want rather than what they do not want; they should also work out where precisely their Object Relation can be the place where they can achieve the great breakthrough in their personal development.

CLOSING REFLECTIONS

The theory behind the Object Relations is well founded and extremely well researched; exceptionally precise studies have been published cov- ering its theoretical structure and content. It is, however, essential for me to conclude with two reflections concerning the genesis of the ego, which is described with such precision by the Object Relations. The first reflection concerns a systemic mentality and the second is about the fact that we are not our ego.

The constructivist approach

There is another way of looking at our personality than that which con- ceives of our ego as more or less immutable, which is usually ascribed to the constructivist approach. This approach takes the view that we are shaped by the learning and creative processes in which we continuously find ourselves, particularly when we are with other people.

This means that we are not one particular personality, given that we co- create ourselves all the time we are with those we need to be with. Right now, I am sitting in a B&B in Italy and am engaged in an early-morning dialogue with the young woman serving breakfast. We have agreed that I can just start with coffee, and Luise will show up in an hour's time. At the moment, I am one particular version of myself; had my morning chat been with Elisabeth, the owner, I would have been a different version of myself – and, had it been Stefano, who is Elisabeth's husband and Italian, I would have been a third (and more Italian) version of myself.

This very dialogue – what has been forged between us; the small, com- pletely new patterns that have emerged; whatever I would have revealed of myself (which is far from 100 percent of myself, but just a little part, given the short time it takes to agree that I will take a coffee and wait for Luise); the thoughts, feelings and perceptions arising during this short period of time – will disclose a specific version of me that is completely unique to this situation. The constructivist way of seeing our personality is thus more creative, constructive and instructive in the moment than rigidly perceiving it through the Freudian prism of the ego and superego. Being open to both approaches – that is, accepting that we have, on the one hand, an ego, which incorporates deep reflections of our early child- hood, and, on the other hand, personalities that are fluid and plastic – enables us to avoid being too rigid in our mind-set about ourselves, such that we ARE one Type according to the Enneagram and can therefore excuse ourselves on the grounds of our Type or hide behind our Type.

I want, therefore, to use this short chapter to remind us all that we ARE not our Type in accordance with the Enneagram, but that we can relate to specific patterns and habits that are deep within us (particularly so given that we have spent our whole lives constructing them) and which make themselves most apparent when we are under pressure – but do not define us, or tell us who we are. As human beings, we are far more magical, nuanced, changeable and unpredictable than any one Ennea- gram Type can describe, and it is likely that it is this aspect of ourselves that we experience when we have carried out some kind of personal un- dertaking and are in a position to forgo our Type and recline in the com- plex, innovative, deep and cocreating entity that is a human being.

We are not our ego

I lean toward the view that our ego is the collection of our ideas, stories, metaphors, roles and convictions we have about ourselves. The ego itself helps us to function during our daily lives, when our ability to operate in our roles as, for example, parents, bosses, and customers is deeply em- bedded in how we navigate the world. Without a secure sense of the role in which we find ourselves and who we are, we will tend to feel lost in a meaningless world in which we ourselves have no purpose – or in which the role we occupy has no purpose.

The ego is made up of two structures: the first is related to the fact that we ARE something and the second to the fact that we HAVE something.

I AM father to my son Philip; I AM self-employed; I AM a boss. I also HAVE a son; I HAVE a girlfriend; I HAVE a company. Together, the many "AMs" and the many "HAVEs" make me feel that things are meaningful, have worth, that I am here, that I have a relationship with someone, and so forth. Yet all these are indeed no more than ideas in our heads – that is, that I AM something or that I HAVE something. As you read this, you may well think: "OK, it is true that Flemming IS a father and that he HAS a company, but this could be no more than an idea or something that is only going on in Flemming's head." I am well aware that I am now entering more philosophical realms, but what if it is the case that I AM nothing in particular and HAVE nothing in particular, but that I am sim- ply present in the world in the same way as a snowflake, the westerly wind, oak trees, foxes and penguins? If this is so, my ego will just stand in the way of simply being present in the world, in that it will mean that I spend a lot of time figuring out what I AM and what I HAVE, rather than just being present in the world. Often when I am writing, I AM noth- ing; neither do I HAVE anything. I am just writing and am present in the world in a completely free and untroubled way. As soon as I start to think about whether I AM a good writer or whether I will soon HAVE a book that others will read, that magic moment, in which I am simply writing while free and untroubled, disappears. You too might have experienced similar moments in which things happen by themselves, when you do not toil to get them done, when others are with you in an encouraging and constructive atmosphere, and when you are not concerned about what others think of you, or whether what you are doing can be utilised by others.

We can only experience such untroubled periods of freedom when we are ego-free and therefore do not overburden ourselves or worry about whether we ARE something (or have to be something in particular or play a special role) or whether we HAVE something (or ought to have something in order to be accepted by our peers).

I have chosen to include these remarks in connection with my work on Object Relations because we can find ourselves stuck in our ego structure or in the structure articulated by the Object Relations. In my experience, to a great extent Object Relations can be used to build mag- ical close relationships and to help you to gain a degree of freedom from your ego and thereby also from the normally fixed idea you have about yourself as well.

If you are a novice in working with your ego and Object Relations, you should be aware that, to begin with, you will be trying to learn the theory and therefore be preoccupied for a time working out exactly what the theory tells you about yourself and your close relationships. With time, you will probably find that you can also become preoccupied with the theory and its tools, seeing things rather too narrowly through the prism of the theory. At such times, you might be well advised to put the theory to one side and simply enjoy those magical moments in which you are free and untroubled, in which your ego does not control your behaviour and you do not concern yourself about what you ARE, or what you HAVE.

THE ENNEAGRAM IN RELATIONSHIPS

1. e-edition

Publisher: Think About It

ISBN 978-87-971234-0-9